KU-738-195

LEARNING ABOUT TEACHING THROUGH CLINICAL SUPERVISION

CROOM HELM CURRICULUM POLICY AND RESEARCH SERIES
Edited by William Reid and Ian Westbury

EVALUATING CURRICULUM PROPOSALS
A Critical Guide
Digby C. Anderson

THE CLASSROOM SOCIETY
The Construction of Educational Experience
Herbert A. Thelen

INNOVATION IN THE SCIENCE CURRICULUM
Classroom Knowledge and Curriculum Change
Edited by John Olson

SCHOOL SUBJECTS AND CURRICULUM CHANGE
Case Studies in the Social History of Curriculum
Ivor Goodson

TEACHER THINKING
A Study of Practical Knowledge
Freema Elbaz

TIME AND SCHOOL LEARNING
Lorin W. Anderson

LEARNING MATHEMATICS
The Cognitive Science Approach to Mathematics Education
Robert B. Davis

CLASSROOM ENVIRONMENT
Barry J. Fraser

Learning About Teaching Through Clinical Supervision

Edited by W. John Smyth

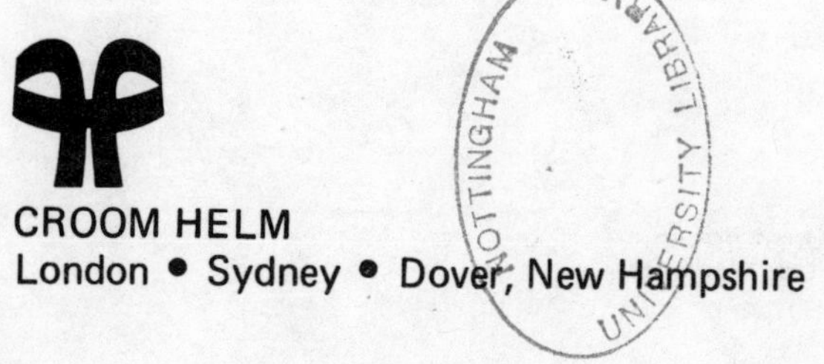

CROOM HELM
London • Sydney • Dover, New Hampshire

Croom Helm Ltd, Provident House, Burrell Row,
Beckenham, Kent BR3 1AT
Croom Helm Australia Pty Ltd, Suite 4, 6th Floor,
64-76 Kippax Street, Surry Hills, NSW 2010, Australia

British Library Cataloguing in Publication Data

Learning about teaching through clinical supervision.
1. Teachers – In-service training
I. Smyth, W. John
371.1'02 LB1731

ISBN 0-7099-4417-9

Croom Helm, 51 Washington Street, Dover,
New Hampshire 03820, USA

Library of Congress Cataloging in Publication Data

Learning about teaching through clinical supervision

Includes index.
1. School supervision–addresses, essays, lectures.
2. Action research in education–addresses, essays, lectures. I. Smyth, W. John.
LB2822.L39 1986 371.2 86-2612
ISBN 0-7099-4417-9

Printed and bound in Great Britain
by Billing & Sons Limited, Worcester.

CONTENTS

ACKNOWLEDGEMENTS

There are a number of people to whom I owe a personal debt of gratitude in enabling this book to come to fruition.

Were it not for Myer Horowitz of the University of Alberta who challenged and encouraged me as a graduate student a decade ago to search for better ways of working with teachers, then clinical supervision may well have been an educational idea that passed me by.

My willing collaborators in this venture, Bob Anderson, Noreen Garman, Tom Sergiovanni, John Retallick, Brent Kilbourn and Lee Goldsberry, are colleagues in the true Goldhammer/Cogan sense; I am grateful to them for their forebearance. Colleagues around me like Stephen Kemmis, Colin Henry, Barrie Dickie and Richard Tinning have influenced my own thinking about clinical supervision for the better, and have provided the stimulating environment in which the present pursuit has been possible. For enabling me to meet unrealistic self-imposed deadlines for the typing of the manuscript and secretarial support, I owe it all to Sylvia Baker and Leonie Taylor.

I should like to thank those authors, publishers and other copyright holders who kindly gave me permission to reproduce material in this book. While every care has been taken to trace and acknowledge copyright, I tender my apologies for any accidental infringement.

Deakin University
Geelong, Australia

John Smyth

LIST OF CONTRIBUTORS

ROBERT H. ANDERSON is President of Pedamorphosis Inc., and former Dean and Professor of Education at Texas Tech University.

NOREEN GARMAN is Associate Professor of Education at the University of Pittsburgh.

LEE GOLDSBERRY is Assistant Professor of Education at Pennsylvania State University.

BRENT KILBOURN is Associate Professor of Education at the Ontario Institute for Studies in Education.

JOHN RETALLICK is Senior Lecturer in the School of Education at Riverina-Murray Institute of Higher Education, Australia. He is also a doctoral student at Deakin University.

THOMAS SERGIOVANNI is the Lillian Radford Professor of Education at Trinity University, San Antonio, Texas.

JOHN SMYTH is Deputy Dean and Associate Professor in the School of Education at Deakin University, Victoria, Australia.

OBITUARY

At the time of this book going to press, the sad news was learned of the death of Morris Cogan. For those who contributed to this volume and knew his pioneering work, his passing will be a great loss.

INTRODUCTION

W. John Smyth

This book has, in a sense, been thirty years in the making - not by me personally, but by a large number of people who have toiled and struggled long and hard in the search for more humane ways of working with teachers. To that extent it has been easier for someone such as myself who has been one stage removed from the major action both physically and temporally, to be able to stand back and view the emergent philosophy and practices of clinical supervision, the small but enthusiastic band of supporters, as well as its critics, in somewhat clearer light.

For readers who may have difficulty with the off-putting title 'clinical supervision', some words of reassurance and explanation may be in order. There can be little doubt that the language we use periodically undergoes transformations that closely reflect contemporary conventions and practices. On other occasions it can be more enduring than we would want it to be. When Morris Cogan and associates in the 1950's adopted the word 'clinical' from the medical profession to metaphorically describe forms of learning about teaching that were solidly embedded in the daily classroom practices of teachers, they were opting for a form of language they felt adequately captured their aspirations for the teaching profession. They were vitally concerned about the relationship between theory and practice and of the way in which theory could emerge out of practice, rather than exclusively being 'applied' to practice as is so often the case. What these early pioneers wanted was to emphasise the fact that hitherto real classrooms and the daily practices of teachers, had been largely ignored as a source of important learning about teaching. They had a vision of teachers starting with their own teaching, so as to develop the confidence to experiment with and try out new ideas.

The fact that others who have come on the scene later have difficulty with the 'clinical' lexicon, is unfortunate. The tendency to confuse the Cogan notion of clinical with the everyday connotations of disease, pathology and a certain degree of detachment, does not diminish in any way the efficacy of the way in which the mentors of clinical supervision intended it - namely, to describe a form of professional learning that endorses the primacy of the patient/client/pupil and the situational context in which this occurs.

Nor should we be deterred by the exclusive meaning attaching to the notion of supervision in everyday language as a process of inspection, quality control and overseeing. The initiators clearly did not have this sanction-ridden meaning in mind. They were more concerned with processes of consultation and collaboration and of the way in which professional peers could assist one another in making sense of the perplexing process of teaching.

In reviewing Goldhammer's (1969) original book on clinical supervision Walker (1971) was able to see its major shortfall as well as its potentiality for teachers, when he said :

> This book may well become influential in the future ... for the ideas are powerful and persuasive, and presented in a form that allows extension and adaptation. The weaknesses ... lie in the psychological nature of its approach, for there are limits to which changing individual teachers makes for better education. There are times when we have to kick the system, to change the schools, not the teachers; but I think Robert Goldhammer realises the moral problems that underlie his concept of supervision ... (p.78).

After almost three decades of experimentation, adaptation, and growing acceptance by school practitioners, there is no longer any serious doubt about clinical supervision being a legitimate way of 'knowing about' teaching. The contributions to this volume are tangible evidence that the process is indeed thriving.

What is interesting about these contributions is that despite the variety of perspectives from which the various authors have chosen to approach their topic, the integrity of clinical supervision and what it stands for are very much intact. At the heart is the aim of encouraging dialogue between and among teachers about actual teaching experiences, but in a way that enables questions to be asked about taken-for-granted (even cherished) assumptions and practices, the formulation of alternative hypotheses for action, and the actual testing out of those hypotheses in classroom situations. There is also the quite deliberate and conscious attempt to ensure that issues, concerns or problems looked at, are ones that are not only of interest to the teacher but are ones that are enmeshed in, or naturally emerge out of, the teachers's daily teaching.

When stripped of all its rhetoric, clinical supervision stands for a number of quite explicit values that have to do with helping teachers acquire meaning and understanding from their teaching. In particular it aims :

- . to help a teacher expand his or her perceptions of what it means to be a teacher, through the discovery of strengths and weaknesses;
- . to assist the teacher to regularly and systematically examine personal teaching to see if there is a match between intentions and actions, and ;
- . to provide the teacher with a methodology by which to monitor the effect of bringing about changes to teaching (Moore & Mattaliano, 1970).

Quite apart from investing teachers with a modicum of control over ways of confronting and altering their own teaching and the circumstances in which it occurs, the aspect of clinical supervision that has appeal for teachers is the characteristic spiral format shown in Figure 1. While there is sometimes a difference of opinion as to how many phases or stages are involved in clinical supervision, at the minimum there are four that are readily identifiable.

Figure 1

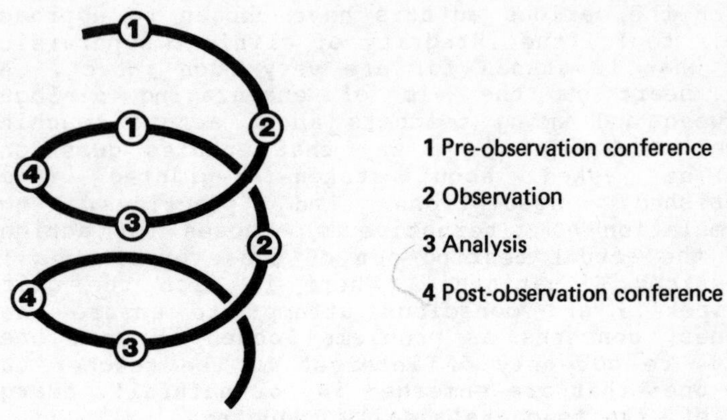

Adapted from Smyth (1984)

The centrepiece of clinical supervision still remains the 'conferencing' (i.e. non-judgemental discussions) between teacher and colleague (see Note 1). One occurs before a lesson is taught, and the other afterwards with the benefit of data collected on the teaching.

In the pre-observation conference discussion focusses upon the teacher's intentions and goals in a particular lesson that is to be observed, the teaching strategies to be employed, the aspect of teaching about which data are to be collected, and the actual data collection method to be used. Throughout, the approach is one of sharing agendas so the observation is as useful and non-threatening as possible. During the actual observation, the teacher and the observer (or supervisor) carry through their pre-formulated plan. Afterwards, teacher and colleague/observer engage in separate analysis of the collected information for what it means, what it reveals and what sense they can make of it. They meet in a post-observation conference to share their separate interpretations of the evidence and to reflect on how the teacher might make changes to practice in some future lesson. Once this point has been reached and possible modifications to teaching canvassed for some future lesson, in effect teacher and colleague have begun to spiral into another stage of the process. There is, of course, another stage in which teacher and colleague reflect on the usefulness or otherwise of the four preceding phases.

A flavour of the historical circumstances that gave rise to what is becoming increasingly accepted as an articulate statement of the process and principles of clinical supervision, is presented by Anderson in Chapter 1. As Anderson unfolds the story we are able to get a unique glimpse of the struggles and frustrations experienced at the time, but we also get something of the sense of euphoria as new ideas were tried and found to work. Anderson locates the developments in clinical supervision in the broad sweep of supervisory practices in the U.S.A., as well as within the contemporary events at Harvard University that represented something of a hothouse for innovative educational practices. What is interesting about Anderson's account of the beginnings of clinical supervision is that while it had its origins in the pre-service training of teachers, the notions soon came to be seen to have wider application to teachers generally.

The latter is taken up by Sergiovanni, and in pursuing this he argues for theoretical underpinnings that help to explain and understand teaching, rather than simply tabulate and measure it. This means collecting practically-oriented data within clinical supervision and penetrating beyond the surface realities; it involves acknowledging that knowing cannot be separated from what is known. For Sergiovanni, this involves uncovering tensions between what practitioners claim they do, in comparison with what they actually do. He claims that using that hiatus productively should be what striving for a better human condition in teaching is all about.

While the language may be slightly different, the message in Chapter 4 is essentially the same - clinical supervision deserves to be rescued from instrumental and technocratic ways of delivering a service to teachers deemed to be inefficient or incompetent. Smyth argues that when used as a way of developing a critical community within schools, clinical supervision has the capacity to enable teachers to celebrate teaching in a way that poses questions about personal and professional histories and constructively challenge the deadening effect of habit. His argument is founded on the belief that the greatest untapped possibilities for clinical supervision reside in enabling teachers to see how the social, cultural and historical circumstances of their work constrain and inhibit their classroom pedagogy. Even more than that, having engaged in these disclosures, clinical supervision is portrayed as a way of teachers collectively beginning to do something about those disabling conditions.

Discussing the research and literature that has been generated about clinical supervision over the past five years, Retallick, in Chapter 5, provides a revealing account of how varying epistemologies and associated methodologies have impregnated writing about clinical supervision. He claims that it is possible to discern an 'empirical-analytic' strand, a 'historical-hermeneutic' (or interpretive) approach, as well as a 'critical' (or emancipatory) view. While not claiming to be a definitive work on this topic, Retallick considers a number of actual studies that show none of the approaches to be value-free - indeed, each endorses certain knowledge-constitutive interests, while denying others. We should, according to Retallick, pay much closer systematic attention to the assumptions which underpin the various approaches to the theory, research and practice of clinical supervision.

Clinical supervision <u>cannot</u> and <u>does not</u> exist in a vacuum. In Chapter 6 Kilbourn argues that it makes little sense empirically or conceptually to discuss clinical supervision in the absence of actual instances of practice. Under these cirucmstances it is not, therefore, hard to understand Kilbourn's proclivity for ethnographic and case study approaches to researching and studying various aspects of clinical supervision practice. His primary concern is related to classroom events considered worthy of attention. Actual excerpts of lesson transcripts are provided as specific illustrations of the intellectual act of teaching and as an indicator of the need to collect data that permits questions of 'who said what', 'where', 'when', 'to whom', and 'with what effects?', to be addressed and answered.

As a fitting conclusion, Goldsberry in Chapter 7, acknowledges the inherent sensibility and worth of other contributions to the book but asks the pertinent question: 'but, does it work?' His concern is with the practical circumstances, hinted at in other chapters, but that need to be attended to if clinical supervision is to meet up to its advance billings at least in the eyes of schools. His sobering conclusion is that if certain questions are asked by participants as to why they 'are into clinical supervision', and as long as some basic principles about change in schools are followed, then clinical supervision is likely to be practicable as well as workable in schools.

NOTE

1. In my own work I have chosen to follow Cogan's (1973) example and use the terms 'colleague' and 'supervisor' interchangeably (on occasions I sometimes also say 'observer', although I acknowledge that there is more involved than mere observation). The distinction is really between teacher and colleague based on function in the clinical supervision process, rather than having to do with experience, status or competence. Indeed, if clinical supervision is played the way I interpret it, there should be frequent and continual reversal of the teacher-colleague relationship.

REFERENCES

Goldhammer, R., Clinical Supervision : Special Methods for the Supervision of Teachers, New York : Holt, Rinehart & Winston, 1969

Moore, J., & Mattaliano, A., Clinical Supervision: A Short Description, West Hartford, Conn: West Hartford Public Schools, 1970

Smyth, J., Clinical Supervision: Collaborative Learning About Teaching. A Handbook. Geelong, Australia : Deakin University Press, 1984

Walker, R., Review of Goldhammer's 'Clinical Supervision: Special Methods for the Supervision of Teachers', Journal of Curriculum Studies, 3 (1), 1971, 77-8

Chapter 1

THE GENESIS OF CLINICAL SUPERVISION

Robert H. Anderson

The literature of instructional supervision is one of the youngest in education, even though supervision as a function has a long history in the schools and school administrators (in particular) have frequently written about their role in overseeing and influencing the classroom behaviours of their teaching staff. Nearly all discussions of these administrative/supervisory activities in schools have been anchored in prevailing practices and theories about the supervision of personnel in the many worlds of work outside of education: business and industry, the military, governmental agencies, religious organisations and the like.

Commentary about the direction and control of workers can be found in the residues of ancient as well as modern civilizations. Most of the work relevant to our discussion here, however, begins in the early twentieth century with Frederick Taylor, whose name is associated with scientific management; Max Weber, who used the term 'bureaucracy' within his theory of administration; and Henri Fayol, who proposed a tightly-defined 'chain of command' for organisational effectiveness. The so-called management revolution that was generated by the ideas of these men from industry had a strong influence upon school practice, and for at least the first third of the twentieth century the supervisory function was defined as holding teachers to carrying out certain practices determined by administrative personnel within an atmosphere that credited an adequate knowledge of the laws of teaching and learning primarily to those select individuals. These viewpoints are still held by some school administrators, even though at least two redefinitions of appropriate supervisory strategies have held sway over the past half-century.

During the 1930's, stimulated by new theoretical conceptions and by experiments with industrial workers and their motivation, a 'human relations' movement emerged as a response to the authoritarian pattern then in vogue in business and industry. What came to be known as 'The Hawthorne Effect', because of studies of positive worker response to more humane treatment in the Hawthorne Plant of the Western Electric Company, was symbolic of the view, that has recently been challenged, that people are both happier and more productive when management shows consideration for them. What some have called human relations supervision, an offshoot of the democratic administration movement, gradually gained prominence and caused supervisors to deal with employees as 'whole people' with worthwhile ideas of their own and with personal, social and other needs to be respected and, where possible, satisfied. Important to this movement was acknowledgement of informal groups within the formal organisation structure as one means for meeting such needs. High morale was sought as a goal; observational methods were adopted from other professions (especially psychoanalysis); participation and interaction were emphasised. The overall impact of human-relations supervision was increasingly evaluated as negligible, and critics contended that participatory supervision degenerated into a permissive, laissez-faire approach in which a concern for winning and maintaining friendships overrode concerns for task accomplishment.

Surveying American history primarily with reference to educational supervision and management, I find that, beginning in colonial times, the visitation and inspection of schools was at first the responsibility of selectmen (town officers), ministers, or committees of citizens, whose focus was upon the suitability and condition of the physical plant and its equipment, on the one hand, and upon pupil achievement, on the other. By the mid-eighteenth century, these functionaries widened their scope to include criticism and advisement of the teacher. During the latter part of that century the 'head teacher' or 'principal teacher', emerged with mostly administrative and managerial duties. In the early nineteenth century that role was supplemented by the superintendent of schools whose power was at first very limited but whose leadership role grew into a more significant one by the end of World War I. A quarter-century earlier, especially in the larger school districts, officers known as 'special supervisors' appeared, selected usually from the ranks of teachers expert in the new subjects then entering the curriculum. Their expertise resided primarily in subject-matter knowledge, and, as was the case with head teachers and principals, their functions were largely confined to administrative matters and the general oversight of teaching procedures and classroom management. Descriptions of supervision in the literature prior to the period following World War I were vague and general, and now seem both moralistic and naive.

As was true of the other sub-literatures within the field of education, the literature on supervision became more scholarly and specific during the 1930's and 1940's. Among the educators who contributed to that literature were several whose primary orientation was to administration (such as Fred Ayer, Elwood Cubberley, George Strayer and Nathan Englehardt) and several whose primary focus was upon teaching or curriculum (Arvil Barr, Ernest Melby, Leo Brueckner, and William Burton). Barr's particular interest was in the evaluation of teacher effectiveness, a topic that also interested Warren Seyfert. It may be appropriate to note that Barr served as this author's adviser and teacher during master's level studies at the University of Wisconsin between 1939 and 1942; Seyfert was my teacher (in supervision) during doctoral work at the University of Chicago; and it was Burton who inducted me into the dynamic climate at Harvard University in 1954 when I became, in a sense, his successor there. These associations, which no doubt explain my deep and abiding interest in supervision, also help me forty-plus years later to consider the probable influence of their work on supervision as a current field of study.

No current text book in supervision can claim the readership of the original Barr, Burton and Brueckner (1938;1947) volume entitled simply _Supervision_. Indeed, in its second edition this important volume was one of the most significant in the history of supervision. By 1955, when the third edition by Burton and Brueckner appeared (with a subtitle: A Social Process), the field had opened up considerably and many additional authors (notably Kimball Wiles, William Melchior, and Chester McNerney) were advocating, as had Barr in particular, a co-operative, democratic, human-relations-oriented view of the supervisory role. By then, too, the national Association for Supervision and Curriculum Development (ASCD) had become a major professional organisation in the States with publications and conferences making a strong contribution to thinking about supervision as a growth-inducing, analytical, participatory, research-based activity.

In 1963 ASCD created a Commission on Supervision Theory, on which I was privileged to serve. Its chairperson was John Lovell, and it was William Lucio (1967) who edited the report 'Supervision: Perspectives and Propositions'. In his introductory chapter Lucio traced the several theories of management that have influenced supervisory practices and policies in schools, observing that since the 1950's Revisionist (or Structuralist) theorists had attempted to reconcile the scientific-management and the human relations viewpoints by putting elements of both approaches together. This group included Douglas McGregor, Chester Barnard, Chris Argyris, and Warren Bennis. In a more recent analysis Sergiovanni and Starratt (1983) described the revisionist movement as primarily a paper effort, poorly understood by those who would implement it, though the ideas of the revisionists remained important.

Sergiovanni and Starratt (1983) also examine 'neoscientific management' in which the current code words are teacher competencies, performance objectives, and cost-benefit analysis. They claim that concern for highly specific performance goals, often at the expense of the human dimension, causes teachers to resist such an approach. These authors then develop the case for what they call human resources supervision. In my judgment, the Sergiovanni-Starratt volume, for which I wrote a Foreword, is one of the best statements about supervision in the current literature.

Clinical supervision, the topic of this volume, occupies a chapter in Sergiovanni and Starratt (1983), and adaptations of the process are presented as 'fairly well developed techniques with artistic potential' (p. 324). Lucio (1967), somewhat earlier, advocated collegial supervision within the context of co-operative staff organisation. Teachers, he noted, reacted favourably to supervision by groups of supervisors, since group supervision tended to reduce some of the factors (bias, or supervisor incompetence) to which teachers sometimes object when visited by only one person.

I first heard this argument during my early years at Harvard University, where Morris Cogan, who uttered it, was my colleague and counterpart. He was Director of Secondary School Apprentice Teaching, a role he had held for several years before my 1954 arrival to become Director of Elementary School Apprentice Teaching. Harvard then had its Master of Arts in Teaching (MAT) program, which prepared college/university graduates in a fairly conventional one-year program for careers as secondary-school teachers. It included course work in educational foundations, subject-related methods, student teaching (usually in the second semester), and graduate work in the field of specialisation. In 1951 Harvard also started up a program to prepare elementary and early-childhood teachers, involving more courses in Education and leading to a master's degree in Education. Cogan's book (1973) which probably should be regarded as the definitive volume in clinical supervision even though Goldhammer and other colleagues/students of Cogan got their ideas published much earlier, includes discussion of how clinical supervision was born out of the conscientious, sometimes agonising search for adequate ways to plan and supervise the initial classroom efforts of the Harvard apprentices.

It was not until the mid 1970's, when Cogan (1976) wrote a paper on the 'Rationale for Clinical Supervision', that he described certain environmental pressures that led inexorably to the development of a clinical approach: (1) 'salient and debilitating inadequacies in the preservice education of teachers', (2) the underdeveloped state of supervisory practice, coupled with an urgent need to help teachers deal with 'myriads of educational novelties', and (3) the need for a rationale, a psychological-sociological frame of reference, for the professional practitioner. In this and in other contexts Cogan notes the importance of providing support for teachers as they seek to deal with the many challenges of teaching, along with establishing an appropriately analytical approach both to the problems of teaching and to ways of dealing with them.

It seems reasonable to claim that the university faculty members who in those days provided supervision, the supervising teachers in the Boston area who worked daily with the apprentices, and the apprentices themselves were by most standards a superior and highly intellectual group. Whether they strove for pedagogic excellence any more earnestly than their counterparts in other colleges or universities is difficult to say now; but that they did indeed struggle for such success is a fact to which I can personally testify. Awareness of the enormous gap between the theoretical ideal, as they perceived it, and the prevailing reality was a constant source of concern. Being articulate, they often expressed that concern, and the dialogue about 'better ways' was unceasing and intense.

In Cogan's (1973) account, changes occurred when 'supervisors began to team up with students, working more intensively for longer periods of time in more sustained sequences of planning, observation and analysis' (p. 6). He saw the conferences following an observed lesson as 'a careful study of the observation data - a quest for the meaning of what had happened in the classroom' (pp. 6-7). Gradually the process became more systematic as observation skills were sharpened, interactions between and among the teachers and students were captured more accurately, analysis of the prevailing patterns of classroom behaviour became more evident, and the participants became more adept at connecting the observed elements in ways that were both rational and useful.

Above all, Cogan (1973) noted, that the emerging approach helped the apprentices (he used the word 'students' throughout) to form larger planning groups and also to team up with supervisors in observation, analysis, and conferences. It was this sequence of events and procedures that came to be known as 'the cycle of supervision'.

During the 1954-1955 academic year Cogan and I were among a group of Harvard faculty and local-area superintendents of schools who, partly in response to a serious shortage of qualified teachers, developed a new approach to the fifth-year graduate preparation of beginning teachers. It became known, and widely emulated, as the Internship Program. It differed significantly from the two-semester apprenticeship program, which thereafter was labelled 'Plan A', in that it (Plan B) called for a pair of neophytes to staff a classroom under the close supervision of a master teacher in an adjoining room and a professor or doctoral student from Harvard who made frequent supervisory visits.

In Plan B, the would-be interns attended an intensive six-weeks summer school where they served their preliminary apprenticeship in classrooms populated every morning by real students and managed by master teachers recruited from school systems across the nation. Several school buildings in Newton, Massachusetts were rented by Harvard for the six weeks, and the Harvard-Newton Summer Program (HNSP) became the launch pad for the interns. These interns also took methods courses at HNSP in the afternoons. In the Fall Term, one member of each pair was assigned to actually take over a classroom in one of the thirteen co-operating school districts, while the other member became a full-time graduate student at Harvard. At mid-year, the partners switched roles. Some of the Harvard courses were held late afternoons or on Saturdays so that the teaching and non-teaching partners could attend together.

While some of this historical information may seem irrelevant, it does indeed help to flesh out the origins of clinical supervision. The specific circumstances, in a way, partly shaped our actions. First, HNSP could not possibly have recruited enough children and enough master teachers to provide each apprentice teacher with a private classroom setting, even had this seemed desirable. However, both Cogan and I could see the merit from a learning point of view of assigning four, five, or sometimes even six apprentices to each class. By enrolling up to 35 children per class, it was possible to provide each apprentice the opportunity to work with small groups of six or more children, a process that was feasible because of ample building space. More important, every total-class lesson that was taught, whether by the master teacher or by a fellow apprentice, was observed (and often subsequently critiqued) by a team of observers that usually included Harvard faculty members.

During 1955-1956, my second year at Harvard,

another opportunity arose to help develop a major idea: team teaching. A volume edited by our colleagues Shaplin and Olds (1964) portrays the way co-operative staffing patterns of several varieties erupted across the nation in the mid-to-late 1950's, and how the stage was set for one of the most adventuresome chapters in the history of education.

The most famous of the early team teaching projects was launched in an elementary school in Lexington, Massachusetts, in September 1957. To help prepare the principal and the seventeen experienced teachers for a dramatically different form of colleagueship, we added a section to the 1957 Harvard-Newton Summer Program which provided a wing of classrooms and about 150 children with whom these pioneers could work. Enter the clinical-supervision cycle: some of the teachers worked with the children while others either planned or observed; team meetings reserved blocks of time for analysis of practices that were working and those that weren't; everyone functioned within what was intended to be, and usually was, a friendly goldfish bowl. A number of Harvard faculty and doctoral students, some of whom later completed research studies related to team teaching and/or to clinical supervision, recognised in this brave venture the opportunity for extraordinary and vital studies of the newly-possible.

Cogan by this time had established himself as a major figure in the field of supervision, and by 1958 he was in demand as a lecturer or consultant on clinical approaches. The first published work using the term was in 1964 (Cogan 1964), with the first major volume on the topic being Goldhammer's (1969) book. I have already noted that Cogan, a skilled but cautious craftsman, did not publish his book until 1973.

Returning to the early literature in which Barr, Burton and others were involved, I have probed that material with great care and I could not find any references either direct or indirect to the clinical, hands-on approach that is central to Cogan's work. In fact, it was almost unnerving to discover how little attention was paid in pre-1955 publications to the activities associated with classroom visitation and observation, data collection and analysis, conferring with teachers, and the other elements now so carefully discussed in books and articles. I therefore perceive, more clearly than before, that the developments at Harvard were a highly creative addition to a literature in much need of a clinical focus.

By 1961 there were so many school districts heavily involved in team teaching, and there was such an accumulated demand for high-level graduate preparation of team members in a clinical setting, that Harvard and the superintendent of schools in Lexington decided to offer a summer program similar to HNSP, but designed for experienced teachers and administrators and organised entirely around team structure. A new elementary school, designed expressly for team teaching, and a flexible junior-high school provided the physical setting. Fortunately, in the summer of 1960 I had run a somewhat similar program in a laboratory school in Madison, Wisconsin, under auspices of The University of Wisconsin's School Improvement Program, and I had learned some useful lessons about how to train experienced teachers who were not only earning graduate credit, but also doing the planning-observing-teaching that comprised their clinical training. The Harvard-Lexington Summer Program (HLSP), then, profited from the Wisconsin trial run.

To remove any confusion that might exist in the mind of the reader about what constitutes the cycle of supervision, let me briefly clarify. At HLSP, and in the two editions of the Goldhammer book that grew out of it, we recognised five stages in the cycle: (1) the pre-observation conference, (2) the actual observation, (3) the post observation activities of data analysis and strategic planning, (4) the supervisory conference, and (5) the post conference review of the four preceding stages. Cogan (1973) presented a totally-compatible version with eight stages: (1) establishing the supervisor-teacher relationship, (2) planning with the teacher, (3) planning the strategy of observation, (4) observing instruction, (5) analysing the teaching learning process, (6) planning the strategy of the conference, (7) the conference, and (8) renewed planning. Cogan's is therefore a more finely-tuned version of the observation cycle, but not operationally much different.

Goldhammer, who was one of the first apprentices with whom I worked at Harvard, became a Cogan disciple and an ardent advocate of clinical supervision as he pursued his doctorate. When Cogan left Harvard to launch a significant and productive career at the University of Pittsburgh, David Tiedeman and David Purpel served with me as Goldhammer's doctoral committee. Both Tiedeman and Purpel (who was an earlier student of Cogan's) were HNSP and HLSP veterans, and the data base for Goldhammer's dissertation were notes from his service during two summers as an observation team leader at HLSP. The dissertation, in turn, became the base for much of the material in his book, which some consider to be one of the most emotionally and intellectually powerful books ever written in education.

As a side note, Goldhammer died before his book was final-edited, and out of admiration for, and loyalty to, a brilliant colleague I completed that work. About seven years later when Robert Krajewski and I prepared a second edition (Goldhammer, Anderson and Krajewski, 1980), we eliminated the almost-overwhelming first chapter and a substantial portion of the more emotional illustrative material, feeling that reducing the adrenalin content would not damage the basic message.

Adrenalin flows, indeed, in almost all discussions of clinical supervision. True to the onward thrust of the work of the human relations theorists, the revisionists, the neoscientists, and perhaps even the human-resources-supervision advocates, clinical supervision represents a powerful convergence of concern for quality education, concern for the dignity and well-being of the teacher, and concern for intellectually and ethically defensible approaches to educational progress (I was tempted to use the word 'reform'). However, the longstanding, and in my view suffocating tradition of self-contained classroom autonomy, combined with arrogant resistance to criticism and fierce defense of idiosyncratic privilege make the prospect of intense, immediate and comprehensive feedback an unwelcome one for many who serve contentedly in classrooms. Even the term 'clinical', the adoption of which caused Cogan all sorts of grief along the way (see his description on pages 8-9 of his book), causes some temperatures to rise and elbows to thrust forward.

While I cannot speak for Cogan or for any of the others who have shared in making 'clinical' an important adjective in the lexicon of supervision, I suspect that all would join me in acknowledging, as I attempted to do near the front of this chapter, that many aspects of clinical supervision have origins that predate our own births. So audacious a phrase as 'The Genesis of Clinical Supervision' in this chapter's title might tempt an author to understate the contributions of more ancient pedagogues or to overstate one's own. In the foregoing material I neglected to mention that William Burton, who spent seventeen years at Harvard prior to 1954, had an office only a few feet from Cogan's. It is impossible to know what if any influence he may have had upon discussions about the supervision of Harvard apprentices. It is also possible that other educators, in other countries outside the U.S.A., were 'into' what we now call clinical supervisory activities in more ways than available publications enable us to know. I therefore hope that this brief chapter, which provides at least an imperfect history to work from, will prompt further investigations.

REFERENCES

Barr, S. Burton W. & Brueckner L., Supervision, Second Edition, New York: Appleton-Century-Crofts, 1947

Cogan, M., Clinical supervision by groups, In The College Supervisor: Conflict and Challenge. 43rd Yearboook, The Association for Student Teaching. Dubuque, Iowa: William C. Brown, Inc., 1964

Cogan, M., Clinical Supervision, Boston: Houghton Mifflin, 1973

Cogan, M., Rationale for clinical supervision, Journal of Reseach and Development in Education, 9 (2), 1976, pp.3-19

Goldhammer, R., Clinical Supervision: Special Methods for the Supervision of Teachers. New York: Holt, Rinehart and Winston, Inc., 1969

Goldhammer, R., Anderson R.H., & Krajewski R., Clinical Supervision:Special Methods for the Supervision of Teachers. Second Edition, New York: Holt, Rinehart and Winston, Inc., 1980

Lucio, H., (ed) Supervision: Perspectives and Propositions, Washington, D.C.: Association for Supervision & Curriculum Development, NEA, 1967

Sergiovanni, T.J. & Starratt R.J., Supervision: Human Perspectives. Third Edition. New York: McGraw-Hill Book Company, 1983

Shaplin, J.T., Olds, H.F.,(eds). Team Teaching, New York: Harper and Row, Publishers, 1964

Chapter 2

GETTING TO THE ESSENCE OF PRACTICE IN CLINICAL SUPERVISION

Noreen B. Garman

Introduction

Clinical supervision has emerged as an educational practice over the past thirty years. It has survived, if not with a flourish, at least with a robustness which has allowed supervisors to continue to think and act in vital ways and to progress toward a further understanding of their work. In this chapter I shall attempt to trace the evolution of clinical supervision as I have experienced the progression. The purpose is not to argue that clinical supervision is a full blown practice, but rather to use the developments of the past two decades to get to the essence of practice in clinical supervision.

If clinical supervision was created at Harvard in the 1950's, it was reaffirmed in Pittsburgh in the 1960's through the work of Cogan and Goldhammer. In 1968 I was assigned to supervise secondary education intern-teachers during their summer practicum. The University of Pittsburgh Master of Arts in Teaching (MAT) Program collaborated with Bethel Park High School in their extensive academic summer school program. For six intense weeks a committed group of university and public school educators worked together to study teaching and supervision in action. In these years Morris Cogan supervised my study of supervision as I learned about clinical supervision in much the same way as the early Harvard group had done. Each summer, until 1975, we returned to Bethel Park to continue the intense involvements, perhaps a little wiser than before. I was also supervising new supervisors as they worked with interns in their classrooms each day. We all took clinical supervision for granted as a normal part of the MAT scene, in a setting where everyone was expected to be a learner. Reality was that supervisors were in classrooms everyday, meeting with teachers before and after observation, using 'stable' data, theorising about effective teaching and effective supervision as a matter of course. Reflective practice was played out in a continual 'processing' of events. Clinical supervison, as rationale and procedure, was flourishing in the natural settings that gave rise to it.

By the early 1970's it was clear that clinical supervision was an elegant idea that had potential beyond its place of origin. Cogan (1973) and Goldhammer (1969) both directed their writing to a wider general audience by construing the work of the supervisor primarily as technique. Goldhammer's version became a structural model in which five stages of supervision were named. Cogan's stated purpose in his book was to develop and explicate a system of in-class supervision presented as 'the cycle of supervision' with eight stages. Both dealt with rationale, procedures and methods for supervisory conduct, yet with very different orientations. Both embellished the technique with the rich wisdom of their experiences. These seminal works invited supervisors in other settings to try their hand at some form of clinical supervision. In Cogan's words it could 'prove powerful enough to give supervisors a reasonable hope of accomplishing significant improvements in the teacher's classroom instruction' (1973:xi).

Working on the Technique

During this time clinical supervision came to be thoroughly identified with the technique. The stages provided a linear guide with clearly specified steps while the cycle conveyed the imperative for ongoing involvement and continuity. Observation and analysis in a sense became the action research mode necessary to make informed judgements. Colleagueship, as Cogan emphasised, was the basis for the relationship and all we seemed to need then was enough experience with teachers and supervisors to work out the bugs in the system. Chronic concerns appeared regularly at various phases of the cycle with new supervisors:

(a) PREOBSERVATION CONFERENCE: When new supervisors approached teachers with questions like: 'What do you want me to do for you?' or 'What would you like me to look for?' teachers were not ready for the initiative. They often expressed frustration. Supervisors, they would say, ought to know what to look for. On the other hand, if supervisors approached the conference with :'Tell me what your objectives for the lesson are', the teachers often grumbled about using the conference only for giving information to the supervisor. Many problems emerged because neither the supervisor nor the teacher had a common agreement about the productive use of the preobservation conference.

(b) OBSERVATION: Collecting accurate records of classroom events continued to plague supervisors. It was much easier to use checklists of desired performance or interaction analysis instruments than to generate piles of raw data. In my own studies of new supervisors I was convinced that 'stable data' was essential, especially as a training aspect of their learning (Garman, 1984). The realisation that collecting classroom data was time consuming and cumbersome was not enough reason to alter the procedures.

(c) ANALYSIS: Analysing the piles of data presented its own challenge. Finding patterns in the data and doing a full-blown analysis was especially difficult for those who had narrow images of teaching. Cogan advocated an inductive approach to analysis and would describe it as 'resonating off of the data: to find the significant patterns'. Most new supervisors, however, lacked a language of teaching, particularly the concepts of teaching to attach labels to patterns. They would often select a critical incident in the data and hope it wasn't idiosyncratic (or worse, trivial).

(d) STRATEGY: Although this was presented as a way to pull loose ends together and plan for the conference, the strategy stage was often combined with the overwhelming task of analysis. In the rush of everyday demands planning for a conference was not given a major emphasis. Another perplexing problem for supervisors was the view that teachers should also have done an analysis of the data and prepared a plan for the conference prior to the meeting. This part of the system was often ignored or dealt with perfunctorily in the conference. It was hard enough for supervisors to put the data in usable form and to do a meaningful analysis without having to get the teacher to do the same thing.

(e) CONFERENCE: The conference was an awkward entity. Much thoughtful energy was spent trying to make it less awkward and more productive. Opening lines were tested with regularity, such as: 'How did you feel about the lesson?' Supervisors privately admitted that this gave them the chance to 'get their bearings' in the conference while the teacher talked, and at times, lead the direction of the conference away from critical issues. Often teachers would say they 'jumped in with self-critical remarks to beat the supervisor to the negative comments about he lesson'. At some point in time the indirect approach to a conference format became popular and supervisors began asking more questions and offering less advice. Often the results of the indirect method resembled gentle, soft-spoken interrogation. The ultimate goal was to get the teacher to arrive at his/her own useful ideas, but always there was the unspoken fear of the trivial. While supervisors were preoccupied with learning the complexities of the technique, they were often willing to accept superficial results without asking for and searching out meanings.

In these early years we accepted the technique as being the major thrust of clinical supervision. The difficulties with the process were destructive only if new supervisors did not give themselves enough practice and did not have the resolve to work out apparent difficulties. If they did, we were certain that they could become skillful clinical supervisors. Many did.

When Morris Cogan published his book in 1973 I was asked to review it for a faculty seminar. It was at this time that I began to realise that the technique was not the sole essence of practice. What I called 'the clinical spirit' (Garman, 1982) included philosophic dimensions that had to do with a deep concern for the developing practitioner (supervisor and teacher), with the greatest of respect for their potential. I recognised the necessity for achieving a delicate balance between the authority based upon institutional needs and the autonomy and rights of the individuals. I saw clinical supervision as capable of serving that duality. While my review of the Cogan text was for the most part, enthusiastic, there was a persistent, nagging issue which Cogan had not addressed adequately. My concern was the end purpose to which clinical supervision was directed. The standard answer, that supervision is directed toward the improvement of instruction, seemed banal at best and illogical. It was clear that we had no prescriptions for effective teaching beyond the common sense level of judgement. Cogan's (1975) general goal for clinical supervision was toward the professional development of the teacher. My concern was that we were talking about one group of practitioners (supervisors) who were responsible for developing (or improving) the practice of another group of practitioners (teachers). This seemed like a thoroughly presumptuous idea, especially since the major tenets of clinical supervision focussed on the techniques of supervisory practice, with no mention of instructional theories. The larger issues such as this seemed fraught with anomalies.

Adapting the Original Technique: Issues of Context

In the years that followed the concern with technique the appeal of clinical supervision was clearly in two major contexts: supervision as conducted by administrators in public schools, and university supervisors in teacher education programs. On the surface clinical supervision seemed like a good system for administrators for several reasons. First, superintendents saw the cycle of supervision as a way of involving principals and other supervisory staff in face-to-face evaluation of teaching. The conference stage forced the administrator to face the teacher rather than rely on a purely written evaluation. Second, supervision as classroom visitation, prescription and judgement had long been ritualised in the culture of schools. Clinical supervision legitimated this ritual as good educational practice (Garman, 1985). Third, administrative evaluation became central to clinical supervision and the terms formative and summative evaluation somehow justified the process by tying them to the notion of the improvement of instruction. Fourth, the stages of clinical supervision, as steps, gave a concrete protocol for in-service training for supervisory staff. One of the major arguments in the public school context centered around the question of whether the administrator/evaluator could be doing genuine clinical supervision while also making critical administrative decisions about the teacher. Contradictions of this kind in this context were ever present.

Meanwhile, traditional teacher education programs seemed to provide a more congenial context for clinical supervision. Perhaps this was more to do with aspiration than reality. Field based student teaching represented a place where university supervisors and co-operating teachers could indeed work clinically with student teachers. This might indeed nourish the original notion of technique. Often the conventions within this context of school/university collaboration prevented much serious work in clinical supervision. University supervisors, were frequently busy doctoral students who visited schools once a week and acted primarily as the university representative who co-ordinated programmatic concerns (Zimpher, de Voss & Nott, 1980). For the most part competence in clinical supervision was not a prime concern; it was the co-operating teachers who planned and observed regularly. The co-operating teachers, tended to use their supervisory roles and the responsibility attaching to it to enculturate and socialise student teachers into school routines (Zeichner, 1980).

During the decade of the 1970's clinical supervision, therefore, found support in the contexts of public school settings and teacher education programs. It was an uneasy coalition between the process and its use, and adaptations continued to surface and gain popular support.

Beyond Technique

By the beginning of the 1980's there was a respectable amount of writing on the subject of clinical supervision. A number of papers reflected the state of the art (Reavis, 1978; Sullivan, 1980). Anderson (1) and Krajewski (1980) updated the original Goldhammer work and Acheson and Gall (1980) wrote a popular 'how-to' book. Representing a growing international interest in clinical supervision, Smyth published several scholarly articles as well as a handbook

(Smyth 1984a) and a series of case studies (Smyth 1984b). At the same time a new generation of scholars in teacher education began to study various issues in field based experiences using clinical supervision as an alternative to the conventional type of supervision in teacher education (Zimpher, 1985). The extent of scholars and practitioners in the area is now so extensive as to make documentation in one piece of writing almost impossible. Perhaps this is an indicator of the efficacy of the system.

There is little doubt that the emphasis on technique, inherent in the early work in clinical supervision is still powerful. Notwithstanding, there is a growing recognition that clinical supervision represents a radically different kind of supervision which focusses on intense and productive involvements, where the supervisor has skill and wisdom to bring to an alliance, and where both the teacher and the supervisor willingly strive toward competence. There are others, like Guditus (1982) who suggest that clinical supervision makes a lot of sense from a 'theoretical standpoint', but that it will never become standard practice in the schools because school administrators are already hard pressed for time and don't need the 'added time burden of the clinical approach to supervision'. Despite these practical difficulties, the interest in clinical supervison has in no way diminished. Perhaps clinical supervision represents something of a prototype, a way of reminding educators of the need for competent supervisory practice and what it takes to get there.

It may be that we are about to transcend the preoccupation with technique and discover what the essence of practice might represent beyond the method. Sergiovanni (1976) sounded the challenge when he wrote:

> I believe that clinical supervision at present is too closely associated with a workflow - a pattern of action, and not associated enough with a set of concepts from which a variety of patterns could be generated. The intellectual capital inherent in clinical supervision is in my view more important than its workflow as articulated into steps, strategies and procedures (p. 21).

Concepts : Toward a Language of Practice

Both scholars and practitioners have begun to contribute to a substantive knowledge base generated largely from their collective experiences. We are at the point where clinical supervision has become a recognisable entity capable of interpretation and action. In my own work I have attempted to explicate a beginning conceptual framework from which to derive alternative methods (Garman, 1982). Through this I hope to capture the essence of the original notions, keeping in mind the inconsistencies which have surfaced over the years as the techniques were practiced by different people in different contexts. The concepts, of colleagiality, collaboration, skilled service, and ethical conduct are the imperatives that, when explicated, stake out the domain of the clinical approach to supervision. Colleagiality refers to the posture of the persons who become involved in supervision; their state of being, their prevailing tendencies, or the 'mental baggage' they bring with them as they work together. Collaboration addresses the nature of their involvement during the supervisory alliance. Skilled service is the facility the supervisor is able to offer in terms of competent accommodation and activities as a result of prolonged and specialised training and practice. Ethical conduct is the constant discretion and judgement implicit in one's actions. It is through the maintenance of these standards of behaviour that those involved can be confident that a professional attitude will prevail based upon trust and protection. The cluster of concepts, are used to deal with aspects of the events, rather than with the actual events themselves. They are abstractions that emerge from a particular point of view. Ultimately they form the basis of the language of practice because they are used to name and explain critical phenomena within the stream of events.

It is inevitable that a practice that has any kind of resilience and vitality will generate anomalies. These anomalies are the peculiar inconsistencies and dilemmas within the concepts and they form the basis of progress and continual renewal of professional action. It is some of the dilemmas inherent in the working-out of clinical supervision that I want to turn to now.

(a) COLLEAGIALITY: As an internal state which depends on the way one views the world of teachers and students, colleagiality is the particular frame of mind one brings to educational encounters. Genuine colleagiality is possible when those working together can 'connect' with one another to work together. Another form of connectedness is manifested when one is able to identify with a community of educators and the rich heritage of teaching, learning and schooling. Those who work in these ways are less inclined to identify with a hierarchical structure which depends on role status for authority. Activity within colleagiality resides in the mutual recognition of each other's responsibility, competence and desire for learning.

A major dilemma arises when the following question is posed: 'How can there be genuine colleagiality when it is the teacher's performance that is under scrutiny and the supervisor is the one 'in charge' of collecting and making sense of classroom data?' The original notion of clinical supervision emphasised the supervisor's skill in analysing data from classroom events. If the supervisor lacks the ability to analyse the teaching-learning situation there is a good chance that there will be an unfocussed, muddling around as people work together. On the other hand, if the supervisor has more access to the information than does the teacher, then unwittingly there is a superordinate/subordinate relationship in the making, no matter how well-meaning the supervisor may be.

Another dilemma resides at the very core of adult learning. When one is identified (especially by another) as a learner, there is a social bias, a subtle inference that the learner is subservient, and thus in an inferior or submissive position. Generally it is the teacher who is in this position. If, however, the supervisor is also thought to be a learner, he/she runs the risk of having to admit to having impaired judgement. Being a learner does not fit easily with the supervisor's image. It takes a strong adult to understand that identifying oneself as a learner means 'letting go' for a while.

(b) COLLABORATION: The nature of the involvement between or among colleagues working together is crucial to clinical supervision. If people are resistant or defensive in their alliances they can often interact in a way that reflects politeness, but in which there is a lack of authenticity. In education we are often in these situations. Posturing is a deterrent to collaboration. When people deal with one another honestly, going beyond the ritualistic tendencies to 'maintain face' or give temporary lip service, they begin to collaborate. Collaboration means working together productively.

The crucial question is how to foster these kinds of relationships. The answer seems to lie in changing people's attitudes in order to inspire them toward worthy activities. In doing this there is an operational problem implicit in clinical supervision as it was originally articulated. In the literature the conference is construed as the central source of mutual participation. I believe the conference has been vastly over-rated as a collaborative event. We have put too much educative stock in the conference and have not identified other types of meetings as possibilities. Cogan (1973) was mindful of the limitations of the formal pre-observation conference. He devoted two chapters to 'Lesson Planning' feeling that it was in the planning of lessons that the most serious collaboration could take place. Other scholars have emphasised the post-observation conference, while largely ignoring the planning sessions. In both cases this emphasis on formal conferencing perpetuates the illusion that a great deal more can be accomplished in a formal conference than is logically possible. Specifically designated meetings, such as work sessions (for developing products), study sessions (for considering new ideas and theories) and research sessions (for planning and interpreting data) are not currently part of clinical supervision or schooling, but they make sense if we expect serious collaboration to yield productive results.

(c) SKILLED SERVICE: From its beginnings one of the radical distinctions of clinical supervision has been the notion that clinical supervision is an educational service for the teacher, not an institutional mandate for inspection and quality control by administrators. Terms, such as, client-consultant, have been used to emphasise a 'helping' relationship and then debated because they were inappropriate, contextually or philosophically. In addition the practice of clinical supervision is derived from the assumption that the supervisor understands the nature of educational encounters and has the inquiry skills to make sense out of the events under consideration. Observation and analysis are the conventional clinical functions. In order to analyse the complexity of daily events, the supervisor has various modes of inquiry to draw from, including: discovery, verification, explanation, interpretation and evaluation. In other words the clinical supervisor is knowledgeable about the practice of teaching (from the broadest perspective) as well as the practice of supervision.

A dilemma arises in attempting to find meaningful classroom events through observation and analysis. The supervisor and teacher, in adopting the inductive approach to inquiry, are encouraged not to determine all facets of the analysis of data ahead of time, but to allow for a phenomenological analysis of the events as they unfold in action. Yet the teacher and the supervisor hold substantive theories of teaching, both conscious and inchoate. Theories-in-use and espoused theories (see Argyris & Schon, 1974; Sergiovanni, 1976) cause inconsistencies between knowing and acting. Moreover, one's framework of teaching can become a lens through which to observe and analyse. This is, naturally, a limiting factor and, if one carries a narrow, single 'model of teaching,' all inquiry will be done within a simplistic framework. Broadening one's frame of reference is a constant challenge to a busy practitioner.

One confounding notion in the original clinical supervision work is the assumption that supervisors, like teachers, need prolonged and specialised intellectual training. In Cogan's (1973) words, 'the professional competencies of the practicing clinical supervisor must be learned in an extended program of preparation that includes a carefully planned and supervised practicum, (Cogan, 1973,p.10). In this way, it might be possible to gain the skill which Cogan says is 'too complex and too difficult to master' from reading his text alone. For many supervisors this is not possible. The emphasis however, is still on skilfulness and places a heavy burden on the self-directed nature of the supervisor as learner. The supervisor must be a reflective practitioner and encourage the teacher to be the same.

(d) ETHICAL CONDUCT: Ethical conduct generally implies a belief in the constant exercise of discretion and judgment in supervisory action through personal standards of behaviour. Those involved need to be confident in knowing that a professional attitude will maintain a level of trust and confidentiality. The manner in which we choose to respond to people and situations will continually challenge the ethical spirit. Conflicts and dilemmas are ever present. At each turn judgments can be made based on self-interest, expediency or negativism. We can also choose that which seems fair, good and wise. We may not always know the difference. Yet on the basis of ethical conduct, we are obliged to make the conscious choice.

The Orientation of the Practitioner

The term 'orientation' refers to the specific ways in which an individual looks at the world. Parsons, (1949) points out that the concept of orientation refers to the way in which individual actors define their 'action world'. It includes the notions of point of view, perspective, outlook etc. Underlying every orientation is a definite epistemology, axiology and ontology: i.e. a person's orientation is composed of what he/she believes to be true, to be valuable and to be real (Van Manen, 1977). The concept of orientation is crucial in getting to the essence of clinical supervision. It represents the powerful forces within each one of us that shape our purposeful action. It is in this realm that we take a perspective on practice.

At the epistemological level we are influenced by our notion of knowledge and knowledge use. If we are oriented to believe that techniques and skills are technical and rule-driven from external, objective knowledge then we work to set up models to emulate and test ourselves against. Alternatively, if we identify with the belief that practitioners are reflective, then we use skills and techniques to generate knowledge about our practice through observation and inquiry. In my own work I have taken the view that reflection is at the heart of clinical supervision (Garman, 1984). Other scholars that represent a more technical approach, shape their writing and practice with technical and managerial concepts and metaphors. It is sensible to realise that both positions are viable ways to learn and that, although we may recognise one position, we probably have a strong proclivity for our own preference. It is really a matter of being aware of the existence of our own ways of knowing, and the epistemology of others.

At the axiological level, it is not as easy 'to see the other side', so to speak. It is here that the questions of value surface. That which is moral, aesthetic and worthy of choice become the major focus. At this level our professional orientation will be determined by what we believe to be the mission of supervision. For example, are we engaged in the delivery of services, or do we strive for personal empowerment for those we work with (Fried, 1980)? Do we attempt to control other people's actions, or do we help people take charge of their lives, inspiring them with a feeling of self-worth and a willingness to be self critical? I believe that personal empowerment is the essential ingredient in the mission of supervision. Without a feeling of responsibility for the profession and the sense of empowerment to make a difference, the educator becomes a kind of civil servant in the larger community. Smyth (1984c) argues for empowerment as the major focus in the practice of supervision. In his words, 'to talk of instructional supervision is to still endorse an impersonal, hierarchical process of inspection, domination and quality control' (p.427). Smyth's (1984c) view of clinical supervision is to think of the practice 'in terms of a means of empowerment by which teachers are able to gain control over their teaching as well as their development as professionals'(p. 425).

Scholars such as Smyth (1985) and Zeichner & Teitelbaum (1982) adopt a critical perspective within clinical supervision. They present supervision as a way of enabling teachers to see their classroom action in terms that extend beyond daily pedagogical issues, and in relation to the historical, social and cultural context in which teaching is actually embedded. Smyth (1985) sees the essence of supervision as threefold: 'a respect for the development of the teacher's autonomy; the use of evidence as the basis for all knowledge claims; and acknowledgement of the historical and contemporaneous nature of teachers' actions'(pp. 6-7). It is within the discourse of a critical perspective that he believes teachers can substantially alter current situations within schools.

In an ontological sense our orientation provides us with a 'real world' in which we live. Moving from one orientation to another is usually experienced as a transition between two worlds - as a shift from one reality to another. 'An orientation', says Van Manen (1977) 'has the uncanny quality of encapsulating the person who has learned to adopt it'. As soon as we enter a certain realm of thought, we have to make the rules of this realm our own, in order that the evidence flowing from it will appear compelling to us. Van Manen uses the term 'co-orientational grasping' to refer to the situation in which one person partakes in the orientation of another. Co-orientational grasping occurs when the supervisor is observing a lesson and, for that time, suspends his/her beliefs in ordinary reality in exchange for the beliefs and feelings of the world of the teacher (and/or the student). The supervisor can make practical use of this relationship if he/she manages to arrive at a reflective understanding of the notion of orientation. As Van Manen (1977) points out : 'It is not enough simply to make use of an orientation. One must understand the experience of having an orientation and of having a specific one'(p.213). Likewise, the teacher must also know what the meaning of orientation is and how it is being used. Co-orientational grasping is built into the teacher-learner relationship. Close examination of an individual's products and actions make possible the phenomenological study of the relationship of the experiencing individual to his or her physical and social world.

From Technique to Practice: The Essence of Clinical Supervision

In this chapter I have traced the development of clinical supervision from what I consider to be the state of a technique to what I perceive to be a nascent practice. I would argue that those who adopt clinical supervision (or any procedural system, for that matter) without eventually going beyond the technique state will probably abandon the system at some point for a more immediately workable process. We talk a lot about the proclivity for educators to look for a 'quick fix' which often ends up disappearing on the next bandwagon. (The tired cliches here may be examples of mixed metaphor, but they represent the most common barriers to educational practice.) At the outset of training the technique provides a false sense of knowledgeableness and helps the novice to fend off the anxiety stirred by new tasks. As a temporary defence as well as an early stage of identification with the role of supervisor, the use of technique should be respected. It serves as an indicator of the would-be practitioner's progress, being used with increasing sophistication by those who are growing professionally, and remaining as a sterile defence to be used by those who are not. Persistent reflection and self-confrontation help one to understand the importance of technique and promote its place in the broader meaning of the essence of practice.

Recognising the context of practice is part of the broader meaning of schooling for the practitioner. People and events create a world in which there may or may not be a place for the technique to fit into the cultural patterns and norms of schools. At this point in time and from where I stand, clinical supervision appears to have a more viable place in teacher education pre-service programs than in activities for in-service teachers. But, as we sit on the brink of school reform, situations may develop to nurture the newer versions of clinical supervision. In any setting, however, the practitioner must have a keen appreciation for the context (through culture), yet avoid being bound up in self-imposed restrictions which, on the surface, appear to limit progress in possible new directions.

Eventually the language of practice must mature. Technique represents the literal aspect of language. We talk about procedures and methods in concrete terms that describe actions in clear, linear ways. Concepts, on the other hand, provide the figurative dimension of language. They are the basis of precepts, theories and metaphors which allow for the critical abstractions of practice and can be articulated in such a way as to give life to new methods. Inevitably, as we continue to live out and reflect on the events of practice, anomalies will emerge. These peculiar inconsistencies and dilemmas account for the vitality and progress in the professional world we inhabit and in the collective renewal of the language itself. The mature practitioner becomes aware of his/her orientation in the world of practice. One's epistemology, axiology and ontology provide the basis for knowing and acting in a purposeful way. It is through this means that we get a perspective on the aspects of practice of others.

Good ideas have a history, a context and a language which are continulally renewed and refocussed through a person's orientation. Clinical supervision is a good idea. In getting to the essence of practice one can find the idea of clinical supervision through technique, context, concepts, anomalies and one's orientation. The mature clinical supervisor is one who has the ability to reflect from one to the other in discovering the professional world of practice.

NOTE

1. When Goldhammer died in 1968, it was Robert H. Anderson who worked to get the manuscript ready for publication. He and Robert Krajewski then revised the original work into a contemporary version with Goldhammer recognised as the primary author.

REFERENCES

Acheson, K. & Gall M., Techniques in the Clinical Supervision of Teachers, New York: Longman, 1980

Argyris, C & Schon D., Theory in Practice: Increasing Professional Effectiveness, San Francisco: Jossey-Bass, 1974

Cogan, M., Clinical Supervision, Boston: Houghton, Mifflin, 1973

Cogan, M., Current issues in the education of teachers. In K. Ryan (ed.) Teacher Education, The 74th Yearbook of the Society for the Study of Education (Part II) University of Chicago Press, 1975

Fried, R., Empowerment vs. Delivery of Services, Concord, New Hampshire: New Hampshire Department of Education, 1980

Garman, N., The clinical approach to supervision, In T. Sergiovanni (ed.) Supervision of Teaching. Alexandria, Va: Association for

Supervision and Curriculum Development, 1982

Garman, N., Reflection the heart of clinical supervision: a modern rationale for professional practice, In J. Smyth (ed) _School Based Professional Development, Victoria, Australia_: Deakin University Press, 1984

Garman, N., Clinical supervision: quackery or remedy for professional development, _Journal of Curriculum and Supervision_, _1_ (1), 1985

Goldhammer, R., _Clinical Supervision: Special Methods for the Supervision of Teachers_, New York: Holt, Rinehart & Winston, 1969

Goldhammer, R. Anderson R. and Krajewski, R., _Clinical Supervision: Special Methods for the Supervision of Teachers_, New York: Holt, Rinehart & Winston 1980

Guditus, C., The pre-observation conference: is it worth the effort? _The Pedamorphosis Communique_, _1_ (1), 1982

Parsons, T., _The Structure of Social Action_, New York: The Free Press 1949

Reavis C., _Teacher Improvement through Clinical Supervision_, Bloomington, Ind: Phi Delta Kappa, 1978

Sergiovanni, T., Toward a theory of clinical supervision, _Journal of Research and Development in Education_, _9_ (2), 1976

Smyth, J., _Clinical Supervision - Collaborating Learning about Teaching: A Handbook, Victoria, Australia_: Deakin University Press 1984a

Smyth, J., (ed) _Case Studies in Clinical Supervision_, Victoria, Australia: Deakin University Press, 1984b

Smyth, J., Toward a 'critical consciousness' in the instructional supervision of experienced teachers, _Curriculum Inquiry_, _14_ (4), 1984c

Smyth, J., An alternative and critical perspective for clinical supervision in schools. In Sirotnik K, & Oakes J. (eds.), _Critical Perspectives on the Organisation and Improvement of Schooling_. Mass: Kluwer-Nijhoff, 1985

Sullivan, C., _Clinical Supervision: State of the Art Review_, Alexandria Va.: Association for Supervision and Curriculum Development, 1980

Van Manen, M., Linking ways of knowing with ways of being practical, _Curriculum Inquiry_, _6_, (3), 1977

Zeichner, K., Myths and realities: field-based

experiences in pre-service teacher education. Journal of Teacher Education, 31 (6), 1980

Zeichner K. & Teitelbaum K., Personalized and inquiry-oriented teacher education. An analysis of two approaches to the Development of Curriculum for field-based experiences, Journal of Education for Teaching, 8,(2), 1982

Zimpher, N., deVoss G. & Nott, D., A closer look at university student teacher supervision, Journal of Teacher Education, 31, 1980

Zimpher, N., Current trends in research on university supervision of student teaching. Chapter prepared for a texbook to be edited by Haberman and Backus, 1985

Chapter 3

A THEORY OF PRACTICE FOR CLINICAL SUPERVISION

Thomas J. Sergiovanni

Introduction

One important difference between professional work and that of craftspersons, paraprofessionals and bureaucrats is that professionals rely on informed judgments as they tailor their practice to fit unique situations. Professional knowledge is created in use as professionals practice. Informed judgment, creation of knowledge in use, and skilful use of this knowledge are enhanced and expanded by theory; theory which enlarges one's vision, increases one's understanding and which provides an array of professional practice maps to guide practice. Craftspersons, paraprofessionals and bureaucrats, by contrast, seek to develop highly reliable practice routines for use in situations assumed to be standard and rely heavily on 'pigeonholing' (Mintzberg, 1979) these situations, then drawing on the proper routine.

Clinical supervisory practice is at an important crossroad. In recent years, its knowledge base has expanded and its ideas have become increasingly accepted in practice. Will it evolve into a field of professional practice? Or will it be codified into a set of routines for use in the tradition of craftspersons, paraprofessionals and bureaucrats? The former alternative requires that attention be given to developing a useful and fitting theoretical base. The intent of this chapter is to raise for consideration issues which might facilitate that effort. What kind of theory is appropriate for clinical supervisory practice? What dimensions need to be included in this theory for it to be useful and fitting ?

Theories come in different shapes and sizes,

each having different uses and different purposes. Some theories are highly descriptive, emphasising what is going on, how things work, how predictions can be made and how understanding can be increased. Other theories are highly normative, reflecting a concern for what ought to be, what should happen, what values should dominate, what relationships and situations are good, right and just given the individuals and circumstances involved.

Within the natural sciences, both normative and descriptive theories are important but are pursued separately. Scientists theorise and research with the intent to expand the fund of knowledge. How this knowledge might be used and its effect on humankind raise important value issues and ethical questions which are addressed separately from the original theorising and researching.

Within the human sciences and particularly within professional practice fields (such as medicine, education, and clinical psychology), normative and descriptive theories are much more intertwined. Clinical supervision theory, for example, is concerned with building cognitive maps of explanation and understanding which can help improve professional practice with enhanced teaching and learning as the ultimate goal. The key actors in this enterprise are teachers and supervisors. Their feelings and the circumstances they experience count. Standards of human dignity and justice exist which allow judgements about the appropriateness of these experienced feelings and circumstances. Tension exists between certain practices established as 'effective' by descriptive theory and research and the effects of these practices on teachers and supervisors. A particular practice strategy may work but may not be appropriate given these standards.

Developing a theory of practice in clinical supervision, therefore, requires that one be concerned about establishing 'truth' with respect to effective practice on the one hand and 'appropriateness' of this truthful practice on the other. Let's begin this inquiry into the development of a theory of practice for clinical supervision by examining the issue of establishing truthfulness first. The issue of appropriateness will be considered subsequently.

The Nature of Reality

One measure of truthfulness is whether what is supposed to be true reflects reality. Within descriptive theories, two levels of reality can be differentiated - a configuration level and a meaning level. Configuration reality refers to verifiable descriptions of what is and is constructed from 'brute' data (Taylor, 1971, p.1). Meaning reality refers to what the events which comprise configuration reality mean to people involved and is constructed from sense data (Taylor, 1971, p.5).

In establishing configuration reality within supervision and evaluation, the emphasis is on describing a classroom's features or features of teaching and learning and their factual basis. What are the facts of teaching and its observed or otherwise documented effects in a given classroom? For example, a carefully constructed teaching objective, a set of criterion-referenced test questions and student response data; an accurate record of teacher 'moves' on a classroom evaluation chart; a data display depicting how students spend time; a transcript or 'script tape' of the teacher's lecture designed to assess use of advanced organisers; a recording of student winks, smiles, nods and frequency of hand waving are all teaching facts. Evaluation which seeks to determine teaching facts relies heavily on collecting brute data. By contrast, in establishing meaning reality, the emphasis is on developing the meanings of teaching facts to an individual or a group. What are the meanings of a particular classroom event or several events to the teacher, supervisor or students?

Teaching facts, as determined by brute data, are often the starting point in an evaluation. But brute data cannot stand alone and still have sense in a particular teaching context any more than a word can stand alone from its context or a colour from its field. Yellow, for example, is a colour quite different against a field of white than black. And so it is with brute teaching data recorded from classroom activity. Observation A, when combined with B, may have quite a different meaning and significance than when combined with C. For brute data to become sensible, they must be interpreted in the light of particular circumstances and their meanings to people must be identified.

A Theory of Practice

Perhaps the case for emphasising interpretation and meaning in supervision can be made by paraphrasing an allegory attributed to Ichheiser (cited in Bauman, 1978, p.106). Suppose there is a windowless classroom with three doors, A,C,B; next to each door is a switch; the switch by door A puts on a green light, the switch by door B, a red light, the switch by door C, a blue light; suppose that students, teacher, and supervisor enter the room often, each always using the same door but never the door of the others; students use door A, teachers use door B, and supervisor, door C. Each of the parties will firmly believe, and have evidence which substantiates her or his belief, that the room is a specific colour. Is it the task of the supervisor in this case to establish the facts as she or he sees them? What is truth and what facts exist in this instance? No matter how carefully the supervisor builds a case, truth and fact cannot be separated from the meanings and realities of each of the participants involved in this allegory. And such is the case, as well, in the real world of supervision.

In sum, two types of theories of importance to clinical supervision have been identified: descriptive and normative. Descriptive theories are concerned with what is and normative theories with what ought to be. In establishing what is, two kinds of reality need to be considered: configuration reality and meaning reality. Configuration reality is concerned with teaching facts verified by brute data. Meaning reality is concerned with teaching meanings comprised of sense data. Sense data are brute data interpreted in light of the perception, intentions, and felt effects of those involved in the teaching and supervision under consideration.

A Practical Perspective

Clinical supervisory theory can be developed using a highly theoretical perspective or a more practical one. Given the assumptions provided above, developing a theory designed to inform professional practice requires that one emphasise a practical perspective. A theoretical perspective, by contrast, seeks to establish a true rendering of what is without regard to meaning interpretation or to normative issues. This perspective is measurement oriented, and within it, precision, reliability, construct validity and objectivity are presumed to be of critical importance. A theoretical perspective seeks to establish objective truth about classroom happenings beyond question.

Despite its appeal, a theoretical perspective for supervision provides an unrealistic view and thus is not very useful for guiding practice. Supervision and evaluation, for example, is viewed as a logical process which relies heavily on action strategies based on universal principles, linear thinking, and rational analysis. These strategies assume that supervisory practice is characterised by stability and uniformity of problems, and thus standard practice prescriptions and treatments for working with teachers are appropriate.

In practice, supervision differs markedly from this theoretical view. Patterns of practice are actually characterised by a great deal of uncertainty, instability, complexity and variety. Value conflicts and uniquenesses are accepted aspects of educational settings. These characteristics are, according to Schon (1983, p.14), perceived to be central to the world of professional practice and all the major professions. Because of this centrality, Schon concludes that 'professional knowledge is mismatched to the changing characteristics of the situations of practice' (Schon, 1983, p.14). Though one may be comfortable in viewing supervision as a logical process of problem-solving, a more accurate view may be that it is a process of 'managing messes' (Schon, 1983, p.16). In reality, the task of the supervisor is to make sense of messy situations by increasing understanding and discovering and communicating meanings.

Since situations of practice are characterised by unique events, uniform answers to problems are not likely to be very helpful. Since teachers, supervisors, and students bring to the classroom beliefs, assumptions, values, opinions, and preferences, objective and value-free supervisory strategies are not likely to address issues of importance. Since uncertainty and complexity are normal aspects of the process of teaching, intuition becomes necessary to fill in between the gaps of what can be specified as known. Since reality in practice does not exist separate from persons involved in the process of teaching and supervising, knowing cannot be separated from what is known. Since evaluation reality is linked to the observer and to decisions she or he makes about methods of observation, it is construed as an artifact of the situation. Since supervisory messes are content bound and situationally determined, the practical language of actual classroom life and actual teaching events will be listened to rather than theoretical language or language which may be inherent in rating scales and other measurement devices.

The Clinical Mind in Supervision and Teaching

The crux of the mismatch between professional knowledge conceived as theoretical and actual practice is that teachers operate in a clinical rather than theoretical mode. Hogben (1982), for example, maintains that teachers and other professionals view their work quite differently than do theoreticians or researchers. They have, he concludes, a different world view. He draws his conclusions from Freidson's (1972) extensive examination of the profession of medicine and accepts for teachers the concept of 'clinical mentality' as advanced by Freidson. He concludes that professionals are possessed by a clinical mentality which provides them with a perspective of work at odds with the theoretical perspective.

As part of his analysis, Freidson identifies four major differences. First, professionals aim at action, not at knowledge. Doing something, indeed anything, is always preferable to doing nothing. As they practice, for example, teachers and supervisors are more likely to take action when faced with a problem they don't understand than to wait for theory and research or for a supervisor to unravel the problem. They prefer action over inaction even when such action has little chance of success. In this action process, supervisors and teachers are more likely to seek 'useful' than 'truthful' knowledge and to engage in a process of understanding-seeking rather than truth-seeking. Useful knowledge and increased understanding are prized because they support action.

A truth-seeking approach to supervision would seek to establish and define a single concept of 'good' teaching to be used as a standard for developing and applying measurement rods to determine the extent to which good teaching exists. Despite claims to the contrary, a single concept of good teaching cannot be established empirically and such a concept cannot exist in an absolute sense. Indeed different versions of good teaching exist, each depending upon a different world view, different interests and different purposes. It is possible to agree on a version of good teaching. This agreement would depend not so much on facts or empirically established reality but on a process of justification. Justification, in turn, is a product of our values and interests.

The second characteristic of the clinical mind is that professionals need to believe in what they are doing as they practice. They need to believe that professional action does more good than harm and that they are effective in solving problems and serving clients. Teachers, Hogben (1982) concludes: 'must strongly believe in what they are doing, because their daily practices and decisions are rarely followed by pupil improvement which can be tied unequivocally to those practices and decisions' (p.1). This comment applies as well to supervisors, for they too have precious little with which they can judge their effectiveness. The theoretical perspective encourages detachment and healthy skepticism. By contrast, the world of practice is characterised by close attachment and a commitment to one's course of action.

The third characteristic is the heavy reliance of professionals on their own first-hand experience and on the experience of other professionals with whom they work in similar settings. They rely more on results than theory and trust their own accumulated experience in making decisions about practice, than they do about abstract principles. As Hogben (1982) points out: 'teachers may adopt the rhetoric and slogans emanating from educational psychology, sociology, and the rest as it suits them, but their day-to-day practice often runs counter to theoretical dictates'(p.2).

The final difference revealed by Freidson's comparison is that '... the practitioner is very prone to emphasise the idea of <u>indeterminancy</u> or uncertainty not the idea of regularity of lawful, scientific behaviour' (Hogben,1982, p.2.) which characterises the theoretical perspective. The issue may be less whether professionals want to emphasise uncertainty than that they must. In medicine, for example, a recent review of the research reveals that only about fifteen percent of medical procedures in common use are validated by scientific studies (Gross, 1984, p.27). The figure in education would be even less.

In sum, 'the clinical mind stresses action rather than knowledge; belief in action; reliance on personal experience and 'results' rather than on theory, abstract principles, or 'book knowledge.' And, finally, there is an emphasis on indeterminancy rather than a commitment to the idea of regularity of behaviour' (Hogben, 1982, p.6). It is clear that the clinical mind, and the realities of school practice are characterised by a great deal of uncertainty, instability and complexity. Further, value conflict and uniqueness are accepted aspects of educational settings. These characteristics suggest that the theoretical perspective for supervision and teaching does not adequately reflect the actual conditions faced by supervisors and teachers as they practice.

Developing a Theory of Practice

To this point, it has been argued that the requirements for a theory of clinical supervisory practice are different than those for theories associated with the natural sciences. Supervision, for example, is more aptly described as an 'artificial' science than real (Simon, 1969). Reality within artificial science is created by individuals' concerns and is an artifact of the situation at hand. In Simon's (1969) words: 'The thesis is that certain phenomena are "artificial" in a very special sense: they are as they are only because of the systems being moulded, by goals or purposes, to the environment in which it lives' (1969, p.ix). The classroom, too, can be viewed as an artificial setting whose form and function are determined largely by the stated and implied assumptions, beliefs, and intents of teachers and by their attempts to adjust the classroom to their perceptions of reality.

Clinical supervision is planned intervention into this world of the artificial. Its purpose is to bring about changes in classroom functioning and teacher behaviour. The behavioural world of teachers is, in turn, shaped and influenced by their stated and implied assumptions, beliefs, and goals. Successful changes in the former require changes in the latter.

Within the natural sciences, phenomena behave according to universal laws. The purpose of theory and research is to identify these laws, match them with the behaviour of phenomena (such as genes, particles, or elements), use this matching to make predictions of new behaviour patterns, and to study these patterns in an effort to discover new laws, and so on. The artificial sciences involve human beings, and humans are unique in that they don't behave but they act. Actions stem from needs, motives, perceptions and intentions, and thus have meanings unique to individuals. Whereas the natural sciences are concerned with how things function, scientists associated with the artificial sciences are concerned with both how and why. Why questions make inquiry not only an act of discovery (configuration reality) but also one of sense making (meaning reality).

The world of the artificial is further complicated by the incompleteness of knowledge that one has about oneself and about the world in which one lives. As Simon (1969) notes: 'In actuality, the human being never has more than a fragmentary knowledge of the conditions surrounding his actions, nor more than a slight insight into the regularities and laws that would permit him to induce future consequences from a knowlege of present circumstances' (Simon, 1957, p.81). Clinical supervision, therefore, must not only be concerned with teacher behaviours and the motives, intents and perceptions which are preconditions of this behaviour but with the incompleteness with which most of us view these aspects of ourselves.

Educational Platform

Within clinical supervision conceived as an artificial science, it is not possible to view classroom activity as the logical process of determining objectives, stating them in acceptable form, developing learning experiences and evaluating the outcomes from these experiences in relation to predetermined objectives. This view assumes that teaching is objective and that teachers come to the classroom with a clean slate, free of biases, willing and able to make rational choices. Indeed teachers, supervisors and others bring to the classroom a variety of agendas, some public, many hidden, and probably most unknown.

Typically included in these agendas are what one believes is possible, what one believes is true, and what one believes is desirable with regard to teaching and learning. These assumptions, theories, and beliefs about effective teaching, the purpose of schooling, perceptions of students, what knowledge is of most worth, the value of certain teaching techniques and pedagogical principles, all comprise a person's educational platform. A platform implies something that supports one's actions and is something which one uses to justify or validate her or his actions. Educational platforms are powerful determinants of the nature and quality of life in classrooms. In the world of the classroom, the components of educational platforms are not generally known. That is, teachers tend to be unaware of their assumptions, theories, and objectives. Sometimes they adopt components of a platform that seem right, that have the ring of fashionable rhetoric, or that coincide with the expectation of important others. Publicly they may say one thing and assume that their classroom behaviour is governed by this statement, but privately or even unknowingly they may believe in something else that actually governs their classroom behaviour.

The clinical supervisor, then, needs to be concerned with two action theories that the teacher brings to the classroom - an espoused theory and a theory-in-use. As Argyris and Schon (1974) state:

> When someone is asked how he would behave under certain circumstances, the answer he usually gives is his espoused theory of action for that situation. This is the theory of action to which he gives allegiance, and which, upon request, he communicates to others. However, the theory that actually governs his action is his theory in use. This theory may or may not be compatible with his espoused theory; furthermore, the individual may or may not be aware of the incompatability of the two theories (p.7).

Helping Teachers Changes

If teachers are unaware of inconsistencies

between their espoused theories and their theories-in-use, they are not likely to search for alternatives to their present teaching patterns. One way in which search behaviour can be evoked is by surfacing dilemmas. Dilemmas surface as a result of teachers learning that their theories-in-use are not consistent with their espoused theories. Theories-in-use, however, are generally not known to teachers and must be constructed from observation of teacher behaviour and artifacts of that behaviour. This reality suggests that greater emphasis needs to be placed on developing portraits of teaching, on providing mirror images which reflect the real events of classroom happenings. But since sense making is an integral part of clinical supervision, supervisors and teachers need to go beyond descriptions to interpretations of classroom events.

John Mann (1967) distinguishes between picturing and disclosure models of evaluation by noting that disclosure models contain key characteristics of the teaching activity under study but move beyond to interpreting meaning, raising issues, and testing propositions about this phenomenon. Examples of analogies associated with picturing are legal transcript, video tape, replica-photo, interaction-analysis, electronic portrait, music or dance score, playscript, and historic chronology. By contrast, impressionistic painting, collage, book review, interpretive photo, music dance or play performance and story would be associated with disclosure. The concepts of picturing and disclosure might be viewed as range parameters within which supervisors can work. At times, picturing events as accurately as possible might make sense, and at other times moving towards the disclosure end of this range might be appropriate.

Videotaping is a common technique associated with clinical supervision. This technique can provide a useful and readily accessible representation of teaching and classroom life. But because of the selective nature of lens and screen, this technique can also frame perceptions and evoke slanted meanings. Further, what the screen shows always represents a choice between possibilities and therefore provides an incomplete picture. And finally, some aspects of classroom life do not lend themselves very well to lens and screen and could be neglected. The collection of artifacts of teaching and the development of an evaluation portfolio, when used in conjunction with videotaping, can help provide a more complete representation of classroom life and therefore can increase meaning.

Artifacts and portfolios can also stand apart from videotaping and indeed can stand apart from each other. Artifacts of teaching include work materials, test files, photo essays, plans, notebooks, bulletin board displays, and other teaching products. An evaluation portfolio is a collection of classroom and teaching life. Though the materials in a portfolio would normally be loosely collected and therefore suitable for rearrangement from time to time to reflect different aspects of the class, the portfolio can be designed with a sense of purpose in mind. Like the artist who prepares a portfolio of her or his work to refelect a point of view, the teacher can prepare a similar representation of her or his work. Together, supervisor and teacher can use the collected artifacts to identify key issues, to identify the dimensions of the teacher's educational platform, as testimony that targets have been met, and as a vehicle for identifying serendipitous but worthwhile outcomes of teaching.

Using Evaluation Information

How information collected about teaching and learning is used in evaluation makes a difference in how clinical supervision unfolds. Evaluation information can be used instrumentally or conceptually (Kennedy, 1984, p.207). When used instrumentally, evaluation information becomes 'evidence' which is assumed to be instructive in decision making. For example, a written transcript of fifteen minutes of classroom interaction might be prepared by the supervisor. From this tape, 'the observer can recreate the sequence of the lesson, determine the objective of the lesson, identify salient teacher and student behaviours that were enabling, useless or even interfering with achievement and, from these data, design the objective for a subsequent growth-evoking instructional conference to be held with the principal' (Hunter, 1984, p.186).

When evaluation information is used instrumentally, the emphasis is on configuration rather than meaning reality; on telling rather than interpreting; on espoused rather than theory-in-use; on picturing rather than disclosing - none of which are conducive to sense making. Further, instrumental evaluation information raises issues of dominance and control. Who has a right to do what to whom? Whose view of reality will become the official view? These normative issues are topics for later discussion.

When evaluation information is used conceptually, it becomes less 'evidence' and more 'food for thought'. As Kennedy (1984) suggests: 'Whereas the current feature of the instrumental model is the decision, the central feature of the conceptual model is the human information processor ...' (p.207). She points out that human information processors are assumed to have a good deal of knowledge about the events under study already in hand. When evaluation evidence is received, it is considered within this broader knowledge base. As a result, the human information processor interacts with the evidence, interprets its meaning, decides its relevance, and determines whether and how it will influence his or her thinking and subsequent decisions. In other words, the purpose of evaluation information is to promote informed intuition. Informed intuition enables supervisor and teacher to reflect on their practice with greater understanding, to enhance their collective professional judgment, and to make better decisions about this practice.

Empathy and The Reconstruction of Teaching

Critical to implementing clinical supervision is the importance of empathy. Each person involved needs to be consciously sensitive to the preconceptions, intentions, and motives of others. Further, an additional empathetic requirement is the monitoring of reactions, perceptions, and felt meanings as the process of clinical supervision unfolds. Empathy increases as the lines between supervisor and teacher become less defined and when supervisors live their lives more as principal-teachers, helper-teachers, and advisers rather than as managers and evaluators. In a sense, supervisors might adopt an anthropological stance -- becoming not neutral and impartial outside observers who collect objective data, but participant-observers in the unfolding of classroom life under study.

Clinical supervision conceived as sense

making requires that the teaching be reconstructed for it to be considered as real to those involved, properly understood, and evaluated. Within the process of reconstruction, identifying the object of evaluation and the subject who conducts the evaluation may be more difficult than is first apparent. Traditionally the supervisor is the subject who evaluates the teacher as object. Teaching itself is of concern, but no distinction is made between the teacher and teaching.

An improved conception requires the temporary separation of teacher from teaching and concentrating on the teaching itself as the object of evaluation. Evaluations of this type typically seek to develop a portrait, map, record, and/or data display which represents the actual teaching. It is assumed that teacher and supervisor are then able to examine this teaching portrait in a fairly detached and objective manner. But in any evaluation, one learns as much, if not more, about the person conducting the evaluation than the intended subjects and objects of the evaluation.

Supervisors don't come to the classroom in the form of a tabula rasa. As humans, they bring with them perceptions, favoured views of teaching, and other biases which constitute a pre-understanding of the teaching to be observed and they way in which evaluation is to unfold. This pre-understanding comes to play in every facet of the evaluation from deciding what issues will be included, to what methods will be used and what information will be collected. Ultimately this pre-understanding helps decide how the evaluation stands and what it means. The supervisor, for example, who identifies with direct instruction will find some issues more significant than others and will choose certain data collection methods over others. This is true, as well, for supervisors who identify with more unstructured and informal approaches to teaching and learning. Whatever one's world view of teaching, it leads to certain decisions which stack the deck in determining what will happen, how, and what it means. Evaluation knowledge, then, is not a passive mirror of reality. Instead its nature and consequences are determined by the understanding which the supervisor brings to the evaluation. The supervisor's standpoint, therefore, is initially determining. Once this standpoint is known, much of the style, method and outcome of an evaluation can be predicted.

Supervisory actions are, in fact, self-revelations, a bit like autobiography. To understand evaluation, one must understand the evaluator, and every evaluation reflects the life history of the evaluator. But even evaluation as autobiography is too simple an image to capture its complexity. Indeed the teacher too brings her or his baggage to the process, and this baggage must be unpacked and accounted for.

Evaluation, then is multi-biographical in nature. Taking into account this multi-biographical aspect, the process of supervision might unfold as follows: the supervisor looks at teaching and sees her or himself. The teacher looks at teaching and sees her or himself. Together they examine teaching in light of their self-revelations. Through dialogue, teaching is reconstructed. Reconstructed teaching is born of interpretation and is concerned with sense making. It is allied with personal realities, the realities which count for those involved rather than with reality construed as something detached, objective, or just 'out there.' It is the reality of meaning rather than configuration reality.

If one accepts the importance of meaning reality and recognises the inescapable multiple biography problem faced in clinical supervision, then it becomes necessary for teachers to be relatively free from their teaching. Teachers will need to be able to reflect on teaching if it is to be reconstructed, and this requires participation in the process without the encumbrance of being its direct target. In a sense, the teaching must stand alone in its own right much as is the case with works of art or other creations. This is the point and intent of reconstructed teaching. If properly free from teaching, teacher and supervisor can inquire into its history to discover new facts, revelations, and meanings.

Normative Theory

Theories of practice are designed to improve things, to bring about higher standards, to strive for a better life. Clinical supervision, for example, is not engaged in to expand the fund of knowledge which exists in the measurement and evaluation disciplines. It is, instead, intended to help teachers and supervisors to understand better and to learn more about their science and art and to help them become more reflective and accomplished in their practice. These goals are justified by returns to teachers which enhance their self-images and satisfaction as persons and returns to students in the form of improved teaching and learning.

Much debate exists as to the role of normative theorising in any scientific endeavour. Skeptics point to the difficulty of establishing the truth of assertions which stem from this theorising. Part of the difficulty is the insistence that the same definitions of truth used in traditional theoretical science be used for normative assertions. Paul Taylor (1958) points out, however, that the truth of normative assertions differs from the truth of factual assertions :

> The truth of normative assertions depends on human decisions; the truth of factual assertions does not. A factual assertion is true if it corresponds to the way the world is regardless of the way we want the world to be ... A normative assertion is true, on the other hand, only because we have decided to adopt a standard or rule as applicable to what we are making the assertion about. Unless we make such a decision our assertion has no truth or falsity. And the way the world is does not logically determine what decisions we must make ... We must <u>decide</u> what ought to be the case. We cannot <u>discover</u> what ought to be the case by investigating what is the case (p.248).

Dominance and control are problems inherently built into the design of clinical and other forms of supervision. Though this design defect may be unintended, it is real enough to provide the need for normative discourse to be part of theorising about and practising clinical supervision.

Dominance and control stem in part from the association of the supervisory role with hierarchical authority. The person in authority is responsible for what takes place within the supervisory process. As such, the supervisor too often assumes responsibility for setting up the basic design within which supervision will occur, for deciding what the agenda will be, and for deciding the ways in which information will be collected. Despite attempts to be objective in this process, each of these decisions reflects the supervisor's or someone else's preconception of teaching and thus is biased. As preconceptions differ, so do the rules of evaluation and the outcomes of applying these rules.

Thus, no evaluation method, instrument, or technique is objective. Even the most carefully constructed 'objective' evaluation instrument uniformly applied to teachers is subjective. Someone had to make a decision as to what to include in the rating scale, method, or instrument, and in this sense whatever 'objectivity' exists was decided upon in a subjective manner. Unless the lines between teacher and supervisor are reduced and unless they focus together on teaching as the object of evaluation (rather than the teacher being the object) the deck is stacked too heavily in favour of the supervisor.

Reflecting on teaching requires that an authentic dialogue take place between teacher and supervisor. This dialogue requires a partnership characterised by the usual and important inter-personal necessities such as trust and sharing plus a healthy degree of equality. Teachers need to be liberated as much as possible from the hierarchical constraints implicit in their role if they are to interact with supervisors meaningfully. Supervisors too are encumbered by their roles and need to be liberated. Efforts to conceptually separate teachers from teaching helps as does making less clear the line between supervisor and teacher. But none of these emphases is enough. Needed too will be an emphasis on ordinary language in the process of supervision.

Typically the language of supervisory conferences is too theoretical, abstract and remote for sense making and meaningful use. This problem is a function of using rating scales and technical data collection strategies which impose a technical language system. It stems as well from an implicit power stuggle which exists between supervisors and teachers. As Greenfield (1982) states: 'Language is power. It literally makes reality appear and disappear. Those who control language control thought -- and thereby themselves and others. We build categories to dominate the world and its organization' (p.8). In self defense, teachers often seize upon technical language too and when, this happens, the process of supervision is intellectualised away. Liberation for both teachers and supervisors will not be achieved unless ordinary language, the pratical language of the classroom and teacher, the language of particular instances and specific assocations dominates in the process of supervision.

A Normative Framework for Deciding

The question remains, how might decisions be made within the context of clinical supervision that are sensitive to a variety of interests and intents? This question cannot be answered directly, for situations of context are far too particularistic. But certain normative criteria can be identified to which parties involved in clinical supervision can adhere as they work and plan together and decide courses of action. Habermas (1971) identifies three cognitive interests which all human beings possess; an interest in controlling our environment; an interest in communicating meaningfully with others in search of our identity, sense of community, and significance; and an interest in understanding ourselves and our world. Supervisory practice should serve these interests by emphasising the real world of teaching and how it works; by being sensitive to understandings and meanings which define unique contexts of teaching and learning and which are actually experienced by those involved in the process of clinical supervision; and by striving to better the human condition which characterises teaching.

Ours is an institutionalised society, and the institutionalisation of schools within a political context claims certain interests, too. As institutions, schools must respond to such instrumental interests as achievement, efficiency, legitimacy, standardisation and maximisation. Sometimes these interests conflict with those of persons involved in the process of clinical supervision.

In attempting to bring together institutional and human concerns, Gastil (1977) has suggested that a pluralistic framework comprised of four essential, albeit often competing, value interests be used to help shape and inform the decision process. Two of the interests are concerned with achievement (Utility and Transcendence) and two provide constraints on achievement (Ethical Limits and Justice). Each of the interests is briefly described below:

> Utility: This value reflects such instrumental and achievement-oriented concerns as social maximisation, costs and benefits, efficiency and effectiveness and other aspects of material production. Not tending to utility results in challenges to a school's legitimacy.
>
> Transcendence: This value is also concerned with achievement but is less routine and instrumental than utility placing instead greater emphasis on growth in new understanding and developing higher standards of achievement. Transcendence favors creativity and quality over efficiency and effectiveness.
>
> Justice: This value interest evolves from the principle of full social and political equality in the distribution of societal benefits (Rawls, 1971) and speaks to the issue of who benefits from supervision (teachers, administrators, supervisors, sponsors of accountability systems, parents, students, etc.) and are the benefits equitably distributed?
>
> Ethical Limits: This value interest speaks to the broad array of ethical concerns inherent in the process of supervision (dominance, control, manipulation, lying, etc.)

Gastil's ideas are more fully developed elsewhere (Sergiovanni, 1980). Supervisory decisions and settings would be those which optimally reflect all four of the value interests. However, in the world of real people, events and circumstances, one is concerned with better relative to other decisions and settings. Better supervisory decisions and settings would be characterised by reasonable balance among the four. Two caveats exist when seeking this balance: ethical limits and justice are far less elastic than utility and transcendence and thus are easily compromised; and, a serious deficit or excess in any one value interest, relative to the others, has negative consequences on the others.

Summary

Theories in support of professional practice are judged on the basis of their usefulness and appropriateness in informing practice. Professionals create knowledge in use as they tailor practices to unique situations. Theory helps inform professional intuition and judgement and thus enhances creation of knowledge in use. For clinical supervisory practice to emerge as a professional field, it too must be based on these premises. But not any theory will do. Clinical supervision requires a theory which provides for normative interests and concerns; which admits to both configuration and meaning reality; which acknowledges the different existences of espoused theories of action and theories embodied in use; which accommodates to the 'clinical mind' of teachers and teaching; and which places the reconstruction of teaching at the centre of its conceptual structure.

NOTES

Many of the ideas presented in this chapter are from previous papers and are used without specific reference. See, for example: Sergiovanni (1981), (1982), (1984a), (1984b), (1985).

REFERENCES

Argyris, C. & D., Schon, D., Theory in Practice: Increasing Professional Effectiveness, San Francisco, Ca: Jossey-Bass, 1974

Bauman, Z., Hermeneutics and Social Science, New York: Columbia University Press, 1979

Freidson, E. Profession of Medicine: A Study of the Sociology of Applied Knowledge, New York: David Mead, 1972

Gastil, R., Social Humanities, San Francisco: Jossey-Bass, 1977

Gross, S., On contrasting rates of diffusion of professional knowledge: a response to McGuire and Tyler, In P. Hosford (ed.) Using What We Know About Teaching, Alexandria, Va : Yearbook of the Association for Supervision and Curriculum Development, 1984

Hogben, D., The clinical mind: some implications of educational research and teacher training, South Pacific Journal of Teacher Education, 10 (1), 1981

Hunter, M., Knowing, teaching and supervising, In P. Hosford (ed.) Using What we know About Teaching. Alexandria, Va : Yearbook of the Association for Supervision and Curriculum Development : Alexandria, Va, 1984

Kennedy, M., How evidence alters understanding and decisions. Educational Evaluation and Policy Analysis, 6, (3), 1984, 207-226

Mann, J., Curriculum criticism, The Teachers College Record, 71 (1), 1967, 27-40

Rawls, J., A Theory of Justice, Cambridge: Harvard University, 1971

Schon, D., The Reflective Practitioner: How Professionals Think in Action, New York: Basic Books, 1983.

Sergiovanni, T., A social humanities view of educational policy and administration, Educational Administration Quarterly, 16 (1), 1980, 1-20

Sergiovanni, T., Interpretation and meaning in the evaluation of teaching. Paper presented to the American Educational Research Association, Los Angeles, 1981

Sergiovanni, T., Supervision and evaluation: interpretive and critical perspectives. Paper presented to the Council of Professors of Instructional Supervision. Knoxville, Tennessee, 1982

Sergiovanni, T., Liberating supervision in search of meaning, Impact on Instructional Improvement, 19, (1) 1984a pp. 52-72

Sergiovanni, T., Expanding conceptions of inquiry and practice in supervision and evaluation, Educational Evaluation and Policy Analysis, 6 (4) 1984b pp. 355-365

Sergiovanni, T., Landscapes, mindscapes, and reflective practice in supervision, Journal of Curriculum and Supervision, 1 (1) 1985

Simon, H., Administrative Behavior, Second Edition, New York: The Free Press, 1957

Simon, H., The Sciences of the Artificial, Cambridge, Massachusetts: The MIT Press, 1969

Taylor, C., Interpretation and the sciences of man, The Review of Metaphysics, 15, (1) 1971, pp. 3-51

Taylor, P., Normative Discourse, Englewood Cliffs, New Jersey: Prentice-Hall, 1958

ACKNOWLEDGEMENT

Some of the ideas contained in this chapter have previously been published in *Educational Evaluation and Policy Analysis*, *Journal of Curriculum and Supervision*, and *Impact on Instructional Improvement*.

Chapter 4

TOWARDS A COLLABORATIVE, REFLECTIVE AND CRITICAL MODE OF CLINICAL SUPERVISION

W.J. Smyth

Introduction

A lot of things have happened educationally since Robert Goldhammer (1969) and his associates at Harvard University made their first strident moves to free supervision from its 'watchdog origins' in the 1950's (Smyth, 1985a). What they were looking for at the time was a way in which teachers could work collaboratively with each other that acknowledged the human worth and dignity of the people involved. What is interesting is that despite the rapidity with which educational fads generally come and go, the notion of clinical supervision is still alive and thriving. The reasons for this are not hard to discern. What clinical supervision stands for, in essence, is a view of teacher professionalism that has as its centre-piece investing control of pedagogical matters in the hands of teachers (Smyth 1984a). It is they who 'call the shots' in terms of what is looked at in teaching and schooling and what is considered feasible and practicable to change.

This represents a dramatic departure from other practices in supervision where certain categories of teachers are 'targeted' for treatment - the inexperienced, the weak or the incompetent. The effects of past attempts at supervision were well summed up by Withall and Wood (1979) when they said:

> (Supervision) connotes a situation that is unpleasant, possesses psychological threat, and typically culminates in unrewarding consequences ... (T)here are factors which encourage those undergoing

> supervision to see the activity with a worried, if not fearful eye. One is the manner in which supervisors have tended to project an image of superiority and omniscience in identifying the strengths and weaknesses of a teacher's performance and in offering advice concerning how to improve future performance (p.55).

The major problem with traditional forms of supervision (and clinical supervision is by no means immune) is that they are conceptualised as a delivery of a service to those who need it. No matter how benevolently it is done efforts of this kind are largely self-defeating. Precisely because they are premised on managerial and non-democratic ways of working, these forms of supervision create dependence rather than independence. It is not the teachers' agendas, issues and concerns that are being addressed, but rather those of someone within the administrative or bureaucratic hierarchy. What really is at issue, is the question of who exercises power. As Ryan (1971) put it:

> What some are accustomed to thinking of as the enduring debilitating characteristics of the poor - such as apathy, fatalism, depression, and pessimism - are actually the straightforward manifestations of the dynamics arising from lack of power. Man powerless is not fully man. This concept can illuminate some vexing problems. Why didn't public housing fulfil the dreams of its planners, for example? Or why cannot slum schools educate? Why are so many of our young people robotized by, or alienated from, our major social institutions? The answers to these - and to an almost endless series of similar questions - is the same: we have failed to understand the nature of humanness and to provide for its nurturance; we have restricted people's ability to act effectively on their own behalf - that is, to exercise power (pp.242-3).

Those of us who espouse and use clinical

supervision should be about 'empowerment' rather than the mere 'delivery of services' (Fried, 1980) to colleagues who have perceived deficiencies or problems that need to be corrected. If we are really serious about wanting to change and reform our teaching practices and assist our colleagues to do likewise, we need to view processes like clinical supervision as a way of posing problems about our teaching (i.e. problematising it) in a way that enables us to challenge taken-for-granted assumptions about how we work. In the process we will likely uncover the manifold contradictions, dilemmas and paradoxes that plague us in teaching and schooling.

Since its beginnings supervision of the clinical variety has had a remarkable history in schools. Described as a 'planned intervention into the world of the artificial' (Sergiovanni, 1976, p. 9) clinical supervision has as its prime objective the bringing about of improvement in classroom teaching, although it is concerned as well with 'the incompleteness with which most of us view our assumptions, beliefs, objectives and behavior' (p. 9). Born in the real world of professional practice, clinical supervision arose in response to a concern that ways of working with teachers were ineffectual. The principles, procedures and philosophy of clinical supervision have been applauded by some as corresponding to the 'best existing practice' (Weller, 1969), described as the most sophisticated and concentrated program of supervision around, and labelled by its critics as 'unreal' and 'unworkable' (Curtis, 1975; Guditus, 1982). While I wince at the systems-oriented language used, I believe Wilhelms (Cogan, 1973) had an accurate analogy in describing it as 'a system of supervision with enough weight to have impact and with the precision to hit the target' (p. ix). When compared to the alternatives clinical supervision represents, at best, 'a modest paradigm shift; one with the potential to change the practice of supervision substantially' (Sergiovanni, 1976, p. 21).

Against this backdrop I want to discuss clinical supervision by looking at some of the myth surrounding what it means to act 'clinically'. In this chapter I suggest that we might 'stand off' from the attempts by others to redefine clinical supervision in technocratic ways and return to the spirit of what its mentors had in mind. By drawing upon some ideas from critical social theory (Held, 1980; Bernstein, 1976; Habermas, 1973), I canvass a perspective from which to begin a rethink of the issues implicit within clinical supervision as a way of working with teachers.

The Nature of Clinical Inquiry

The word 'clinical' has a kind of mystique surrounding it (Smyth, 1985b). It frequently conjures up images of pathology and disease, and even worse, notions of manipulation in which something distasteful is done to somebody. As applied to teaching Goldhammer (1969) saw clinical as referring to something quite different:

> ... close observation, detailed observational data, face-to-face interaction between supervisor and teacher, and an intensity of focus that binds the two in an intimate professional relationship (p. 54).

For Cogan, Goldhammer, Anderson and associates at Harvard University in the 1950's, clinical had to do with ways of learning about teaching that were solidly embedded 'in the clinic of the classroom' (Wilhelms in Cogan, 1973, p. ix). They were endorsing much of what Erickson (1969) noted as the original meaning of clinical:

> In the days when the church was the primary guardian of man's well-being, clinical referred to a priest's administrations at the death bed - then the only gateway to true health, since all through life man owed a death. Later, the word was primarily applied to medical ministrations, as science and humanism joined forces in taking the short-range point of view that man owes himself a long and healthy life, or at any rate one free from disease. In our time and in the Western world clinical is expanding rapidly to include not only medical but also social considerations, not only physical well-being but also mental health, not only matters of cure but also prevention, not only therapy but also research. This means that

> clinical work is now allied with many brands of evidence and overlaps with many methodologies (p. 721).

Erickson's comments serve to underscore a number of features of the clinical approach to supervision. First, the fact that clinical pertains to rendering at the bedside - an obvious analogy for the fact that teachers stand to gain substantially from learning about their teaching in a job-embedded way. Second, Erickson noted how clinical encounters pave the way for an understanding of well-being, as well as being used for their accepted therapeutic or curative purposes; for those interested in understanding better how 'good' teachers work, this is significant. Thirdly, Erickson is expansive about what he considers count as methodology and evidence in clinical work - it can include the empirical, observable and verifiable, as well as intuition, interpretation, and the emotional. Finally, there is the importance of incorporating in a mainstream way the views and interpretations of the client/patient 'often making the 'patient himself' an assistant observer and associate doctor' (p. 722). In the Goldhammer (1969) scheme this has its parallel in the well-entrenched view of teachers' autonomy to 'call the shots' in analysing their own teaching.

Freidson (1972) has argued that in certain professions, and I would claim teaching is one of them, it is possible to talk about a 'clinical mentality'. Freidson (1972) sees this as embodying a number of important notions. If I can summarise his argument, briefly; Sergiovanni in this volume gives somewhat more detail.

Firstly, clinical practitioners are more concerned with action than they are with knowledge about their activities, per se. When teachers encounter a problem they are likely to act rather than seek out some empirical solution. Their emphasis is upon 'useful' or practical knowledge, because of the way in which it helps them understand action. For example, teachers are more likely to define teaching in terms of values that express 'what works for us', than they are to rely on empirical research done by somebody outside of schools. Teachers are likely to justify practices based on these experiences. Secondly, professionals who have a clinical mentality emphasise a belief, sometimes quite passionately, in the 'rightness' of what they do. They hold the view that their actions actually lead to the enhancement of the well-being of their clients. Put quite simply, teachers:

> ... must strongly believe in what they are doing, because their daily practices and decisions are rarely followed by pupil improvement which can be tied unequivocally to those practices and decisions (Hogben, 1982, p.1).

Thirdly, clinicians place a heavy emphasis on their own experience, or that of their colleagues. There is a tendency to rely on experience. Even though when questioned teachers tend to over-emphasise the importance of peer interaction in their professional development, Chism (1985) found that 'peer interaction is high only in a relative sense, since generally only a low level of teacher development is present in schools' (p.1). Chism did note, however, that teachers had ways of overcoming the normative and organisational constraints which she described in terms of 'psychological support', 'exchanging favours and materials', 'checking out' and 'parallel play' - all of which involved forms of exchange of one kind or another. Although teachers are sometimes seduced by the latest buzz words, what they actually do is often quite at variance with these utterances. For example, while paying lip-service to notions of school-based curriculum development, they still adhere to centrally provided curriculum guidelines. Similarly, notions of 'child centredness', 'inquiry learning', 'co-operative activities', while fine sounding ideals, often get lost in the shuffle of the daily grind. Finally, Freidson (1972) notes that because of the aura of uncertainty within which the clinical practitioner works, his/her world is one characterised by unpredictability and indeterminacy, rather than predictability and lawlike behaviour. In schools, the bulk of what teachers do is not validated by scientific studies - the range and variety of circumstances are too diffuse for that, and despite the best plans they often find themselves acting in responsive ways.

In exploring the nature of professional knowledge in teaching Doyle (1985) argues for the importance of 'clinical theories' about teaching that are not simply derivatives of psychology, sociology or philosophy, but which emerge instead from 'direct attempts to understand clinical practice on its own terms' (p. 13). His comments on the characteristics of clinical knowledge in teaching fit well with the underlying philosophy of clinical supervision. In particular Doyle (1985) had this to say :

> Clinical knowledge for teaching is grounded in the commonplaces of daily events and processes in classroom environments rather than in the problems and issues of a scientific discipline. In other words, a clinical theorist is interested primarily in understanding classroom teaching and learning rather than extending the frontiers of knowledge in a particular domain of psychology or sociology. This is not to say that constructs, propositions, theories, or methods of inquiry from established disciplines are not useful in the construction of clinical knowledge. But the primary focus is on classrooms.
>
> Clinical knowledge is interpretive and explanatory and not simply predictive. That is, clinical knowledge is not limited to information about validated practices. It also includes attempts to make sense of what goes on in the classrooms. Its domain, in other words, is what teachers need to know to do their work rather than what administrators need to know to control teaching.
>
> The argument for a clinical knowledge base for professional practice in teaching obviously has important implications for research on teaching. In particular, it suggests a need to shift attention from features of successful practice to the components of teachers' knowledge about their craft. Although the conceptual and methodological waters in this region are muddy, efforts to push ahead in this direction promise to increase substantially the intellectual and practice power of inquiry into teaching (pp. 14-15).

It is not hard to move from these general ideas of clinical mentality that have to do with practitioners learning about their profession in a job-embedded, experiential and reflective way, to the specifics of clinical supervision in schools where teachers collaborate through helping each other collect information, extract meaning from that information, and use the insights gained as a basis for trialling other alternatives. It is a way of bringing about change and improvement in teaching in a self-initiated, supportive and systematic way.

In large measure this independence amounting to the freedom to choose from a range of alternative perspectives is what Berlak (1985) labels 'liberation'. Teachers are liberated:

> ... to the extent that they are, at the same time, increasingly free to choose from a range of alternative perspectives on themselves and their social worlds. This freedom of choice requires the ability to see one's own views of what is good or right, possible or impossible, true or false, as problematic, socially constructed, subject to social and political influence (p. 2).

Teachers as Critical Dialecticians

The question of how to bring about lasting, significant and meaningful change of a liberating kind in schools is one of the most enduring, confusing and perplexing issues currently confronting us. Seemingly endless amounts of money, time and effort have been invested in tackling the question from a planned, rational change perspective of developing research agenda, pursuing answers to those research questions, and then disseminating and implementing policy based on those findings. Rarely have teachers' own interpretations and theories about what works in classrooms constituted the basis of change strategies in schools. There is a growing realisation (Tripp, 1984; Rudduck, 1984; Day, 1984) that teachers do have the capacity to engage in practical reflection (Elliott, 1976) through the development of collaborative alliances that not only enrich their sense of what is feasible and possible, but also have the potential to transform their understanding of those realities. The notion of teachers being critical, reflective and responsive to their own and each others' teaching, is not new (Smyth, 1984b). What has been problematic since the writings of Dewey (1933) have been feasible ways of actually doing this. There is a plethora of apparently plausible reasons why teachers do not engage in systematic analysis of their teaching - the isolated nature of classrooms, the complexity of classroom life, inadequate time, a lack of observational prowess, anxiety at having their teaching observed, as well as a belief in the craft-like nature of teaching learned largely on the job by processes of trial and error. This reluctance on the part of teachers has been aided and abetted by an educational system that believes standards of teaching should be ensured through externally imposed minimum standards and mechanisms of inspection, accountability and quality control.

That some commentators have been less than charitable in speaking of teachers' self-monitoring capacities is evident in comments by writers such as Jackson (1968) and Lortie (1975). Berlak and Berlak (1981) indicate that educational scholars like Lortie and Jackson do not appear unsympathetic to teachers, yet their comments about teachers' 'conceptual simplicity' 'avoidance of elaborate language', their 'uncomplicated view of causality', their 'unquestioning acceptance of classroom miracles', and their 'intuitive, rather than rational, approach to classroom events', sound suspiciously like a hegemony in which a low-status group (i.e. teachers) are subordinated and dominated by others (i.e. researchers and administrators). Like Berlak and Berlak (1981 p. 235), I reject the notion that:

> the experts in teaching are not the teachers but scientifically trained administrators, or educational scholars who study schooling scientifically (p. 235).

The idea that teachers are only capable of dispensing the 'soft human virtues of patience, understanding and idealism' (p. 235), and are incapable of rigorous and disciplined thinking about their own teaching, appears to me to be an attitude bordering upon the arrogant. As Elliott (1976) noted:

> The fact that any genuine accountability system embodies the view that teachers are able to identify and diagnose practical problems objectively, is very important because it indicates a respect for the teacher as an autonomous person who is capable of improving his own performance in the light of reflection. The fact that this view is not implicit in many current accountability systems is indicative of the low esteem in which teachers are held (p.55).

For my own part, I would prefer to interpret any past reticence among teachers toward being reflective and analytic as signs of the complexity of the process and the absence of clearly articulated paradigms and frameworks within which to undertake the task. Naturalistic research by MacKay and Marland (1978) underscores the contribution of the classroom context itself:

> Classrooms and classroom activities do not provide reflecting surfaces which enable teachers to 'see themselves' at work. The evidence seems to support the notion that the classroom scene, which presents to the teacher's senses such a rapidly changing kaleidoscope of events, prevents the teacher from seeing a clear and stable image of himself (p.15).

Working towards the concept of 'teachers-as-reflective-spectators' in their own classrooms, Beasley (1981) arrived at a similar conclusion:

> Because of the complexity of their situation, the end result (of observing their own practice) may have an amorphous quality that makes reflecting on what has occurred very difficult. Teachers and students may at the end of a lesson, for example, have a feeling that it went well or badly but discussing why this was so may remain largely at the level of intuition (p. 9).

Rather than being despondent because teachers are

not in the habit of acting reflectively, I would prefer to speculate about some genuinely productive possibilities and prospects for the future which may help teachers gain greater control over their own teaching.

When teachers themselves adopt a reflective attitude towards their teaching, actually questioning their own practices (Holly, 1983), then they engage in a process of rendering problematic aspects of teaching generally taken for granted. Dewey (1933) claimed that to be reflective was to look back over past experiences, extract their net meanings and in the process acquire a guide for future encounters of a similar kind. Implicit in Dewey's view was an open-mindedness towards the acceptance of facts from multiple perspectives, a willingness to consider the possibility of alternative (even competing) realities, and the realisation that cherished beliefs and practices may have to be challenged and even supplanted. Elliott (1976) expressed it somewhat differently when he said:

> changes in classroom practice can be brought about only if teachers become conscious of ... theories and are able to critically reflect about them. Teachers would then be encouraged to reflect about the theories implicit in their own practices and cease to regard them as self-evident (p. 2).

Put simply, to act reflectively about teaching is to pursue actively the possibility that existing practices may effectively be challenged and, in the light of evidence about their efficacy, replaced by alternatives. Reflection, critical awareness and enlightenment on their own are insufficient - they must be accompanied by 'action'. As Benseman (1978) cryptically noted: 'Reflection without action is verbalism; action without reflection is activism' (p. 35). The intent is that teachers reach a point where 'the teaching act itself (is seen) as a source of knowledge' (Devaney, 1977, p. 21).

The starting point, therefore, in changing classroom practices is to get behind the taken-for-grantedness of daily teaching (Smyth, 1985c). It means acknowledging the habitualness of teaching:

> What teaching is vulnerable to is the flattening effect of habit. Habit is seductive : it is soothing, non-provocative and anxiety free .... Good teaching is essentially experimental and experiment entails rescuing at least part of one's work from the predictability of routine (Rudduck, 1984, pp. 5-6).

This not to suggest that classrooms be turned into experimental laboratories, in the classical sense, and that pupils become human guinea pigs. Rather, it is to acknowledge that where classroom teaching goes unexamined, unmonitored or unreflected upon, there are real risks to children. Indeed:

> _Not_ to examine one's practice is irresponsible: to regard teaching as an experiment and to monitor one's performance is a responsible professional act (Rudduck, 1984, p.6).

Changing teaching therefore amounts to educationally justifying why it is we do what we do. Just as we need compelling reasons for altering what we do, we also need some justifying evidence for continuing to do things the way we do. If as a result of examining intentions and actions they are found to be inconsistent, then informed decisions to change can be taken. While we may not have an immediate blueprint of how we intend to operate differently, we have at least begun the difficult process of isolating what should be potential sources of unease. The beginning of the change process is often an acknowledgement of some dilemma, paradox, contradiction, or anxiety that things are not going quite as they might be.

A problem that teachers frequently encounter in beginning to use clinical supervision in the collaborative and reflective way suggested is that they are often unsure where to start. Although the philosophy of clinical supervision is well espoused, and the procedural steps clear enough, what is not at all self-evident is _where_ to get entry into their own teaching. A way of doing this might be for teachers to capture incidents in their own teaching that enable them to at least partially reconstruct classroom events. A journal or a diary (Holly, 1984) is a useful way of doing that - the record at the time need only be a few hurried lines or 'jottings', enough snippets to allow later recall of the issue and its surrounding context. Most teachers who do this actually use the journal to sharpen their focus by concentrating on some problem or concern they may want to begin working upon, using clinical supervision. For example, one teacher who had pupils working through individual assignment cards found:

> There's an initial rush to complete one card - the minimum requirement. When this is completed, though another card is often collected, intensive work ceases and chatting, with some desultory work, is the norm. Talk is voluntarily kept at a quiet level (so the teacher's attention is not drawn to what is happening) (Rudduck, 1984, p. 9).

For this teacher, this was a way of mapping the domain - a way of getting access to a nagging concern. Having done that, and understood the problem a little more clearly, the option was there to use clinical supervision to collect further evidence that may help in devising alternative ways of working.

On other occasions, what starts as a simple problem to be resolved through a journal entry can lead to a discussion of much wider issues about the teacher's unconscious and unexamined values. For example, one teacher wrote in her journal:

> John didn't finish his work again today. Must see he learns to complete what he has begun (Tripp, 1984, p. 28).

For this teacher, writing about this and sharing this incident with a group of supportive colleagues enabled her to see the problem in a different light. Rather than asking 'how can I get Johnny to finish his work?' she was able to see that a more important question was 'why must Johnny finish his work before going onto the next task?' In a sense it was her own sedimented professional history as a successful teacher that prevented her from asking the 'why' questions. Indeed, why was it that she stopped John from starting anything new until the work he had begun was complete? In Tripp's (1984) language, she was 'teaching on autopilot'. He re-formulated the issue in this way:

> In everyday life outside the classroom we continually leave unfinished what we have begun, so how is it that we are in a position of having to enforce upon these students the rule that they must finish one thing before they can go onto the next. Where did that rule come from, and when is it necessary? (p.31)

The issue is one that clearly transcends the individual teacher and has much to do with the hidden curriculum of social control in schooling.

What is highlighted in these examples is that we sometimes need another pair of eyes with which to view the ordinary everyday events of our teaching. The very ordinaryness of it, the habit and the routine, make it difficult to develop a perspective for change. As Rudduck (1984) put it:

> The everyday eyes of teachers have two weaknesses : because of the dominance of habit and routine, (we) are only selectively attentive to the phenomena of (our) classrooms. In a sense (we) are constantly reconstructing the world (we) are familiar with in order to maintain regularities and routines. Secondly, because of (our) busyness, (our) eyes tend only to transcribe the surface realities of classroom interaction. The teacher has to temporarily become a stranger in his or her own classroom (p. 7).

While there may be some ways in which we can distance ourselves from our own teaching, the kaleidoscope of events often preclude us from getting a clear and stable image of ourselves and our teaching. It may be that a role for teachers' colleagues, in getting clinical supervision started is to 'case out' the terrain, or do a reconnaissance of their teaching. What teachers generally find valuable are triggers or instigating events that allow them to get into an analysis of their own teaching.

An example may make this a little more concrete. Kilbourn (1982) describes a case study in which Linda, a teaching colleague, sought his assistance in using clinical supervision to clarify what was going on in her teaching. She was concerned about the apparent apathy of her students. Evidence about how she fielded questions within her class and the way students responded, enabled a number of 'findings' to emerge:

(i) she tended to select the same small group of students to answer her questions; the consequence was that the remainder of the class effectively 'tuned out';

(ii) from the information her colleague collected about what she said to students, it emerged that many of her directions were open-ended, of the kind 'finish this at home, if you feel like it';

(iii) she had no well-defined follow-up activities and no consequences spelt out if work was not done.

What emerged from this reconnaissance of Linda's teaching was a lack of attention to student accountability. She subsequently decided to work on three aspects of her teaching:

- to distribute her questions more widely and to refer answers around among students to solicit opinions and to thus ensure involvement;
- to be more specific about her expectations to students in terms of what was to be done;
- to establish a deliberate follow-up policy, with sanctions, to ensure students covered appropriate units of work.

Clinical supervision, therefore provides a way of endorsing a quite deliberate set of values that regard teachers as autonomous and knowledgeable, and capable of working collaboratively to expose their own dilemmas and their own sense of the inconsistencies in their teaching, as well as tackling the incompleteness with which they regard their own assumptions, beliefs and values of the wider process of schooling. Goldhammer, Anderson and Krajewski (1980) made it clear that the role of the colleague in this was:

> ... less a teacher of technique and ... more a critical dialectician; a mirror; an occasional collaborator in invention; a handmaiden, primarily to the teacher's own strategies; a travelling companion through whatever directions the teacher pursues (p. 135).

The principal committment of the colleague was not one of monitoring or evaluating, but rather that of a consultant to assist the teacher to accomplish whatever he or she wanted to do.

One of the major problems, however, with clinical supervision is that it endorses an individualistic way of learning about teaching. What is lacking is any reference to socially construed ways in which teachers learn as a consequence of developing critical learning communities of professionals within their schools. There is an absence of reference in Goldhammer's (1969) work to the part teachers can play in building and developing supportive institutional structures of shared meanings and understandings. We find no reference, for example, to the ways in which teachers engaged in the exploration of their own and each others' teaching, might collectively share their reflections and learnings about what is possible through the lived experiences of clinical supervision.

Where teachers approach clinical supervision as a first stage in problematising their teaching (i.e. rendering it open to question), and use this as a basis upon which to extend dialogue beyond themselves as individuals into their schools generally, they begin to understand how the conditions that frustrate them came about in the first place. Sharing the joys and frustrations with other teachers similarly engaged in clinical supervision, means that teachers begin to form critical communities within their schools. Using clinical supervision in this way, teachers become active as distinct from passive agents, not just in changing the technicalities of their teaching, but in transforming the conditions, structures and practices that frustrate their teaching. What is significant about clinical supervision used in this way is that it is not an instrumental way of solving problems. It is part of a much wider generative process of examining teaching, uncovering issues, and working to re-construe them in fundamentally different ways.

For processes like clinical supervision to work in ways that foster genuine colleagiality and enable teachers to take charge of their individual and joint practices, we need social structures of schooling that reflect and permit this to happen. While prescriptions are not readily available on how this might happen, the Boston Women's Teachers' Group (Freedman, Jackson and Boles, 1983) made some insightful comments when reporting on work they undertook into contradictions within their own practices. They concluded:

> Teachers frequently expressed a general sense of efficacy in their classrooms, amply documented by anecdotes .... that was lacking or allowed to go unnoticed in the area beyond the classroom ... It was in their attempt to extend the discussion into the areas outside the classroom walls that teachers experienced the greatest resistance - whether this referred to community meetings with parents, whole-school discussions of school climate, or attempts to link one teacher's issues with another's. Pressure from outside support groups, and federal and state programs mandating teacher involvement, afforded the few possibilities for leverage teachers experienced in confronting systemwide reforms (p. 297).

What Freedman et al., (1983) were arguing for was a sense of being a professional that meant a lot more than 'facing the issues alone' - a situation that frequently culminates in the unrewarding consequences of '... bitter self-recrimination or alienation from teachers, parents and students' (p. 298). They were concerned about moving beyond the bankrupt solution of blaming the victim, namely, disaffected teachers. Rather, they saw the problem as one of working on the contradictory demands made on teachers and the institutional structures that create and prevent their resolution. In their words:

> Teachers must now begin to turn the investigation of schools away from

> scapegoating individual teachers, students, parents, and administrators towards a systemwide approach. Teachers must recognize how the structure of schools control their work and deeply affects their relationships with fellow teachers, their students, and their student's families. Teachers must feel free to express these insights and publicly voice their concerns (p. 299).

A Critical Perspective for Clinical Supervision

One of the major limitations of clinical supervision as it is generally conceived is the singular emphasis its proponents place on the correction of deficits within teaching. It is frequently construed as a way in which teachers can find fault with their teaching and move towards devising ways of remediation. Expressed a little more bluntly it is a means by which teachers can 'turn the blow-torch on themselves'. Given this sentiment it is not altogether surprising that teachers have been less than enthusiastic about the possibilities of incorporating clinical supervision into their practices. While improving one's teaching is a laudable ideal, there are clear limits to how far teachers are prepared to go in masochism and acts of self-denigration, even in the interests of improving teaching. Indeed, while teachers are primarily interested in what occurs in their classrooms, their major concerns are not to do with teaching technique per se. Their interests often seem to lie instead in the broader area of how the social, cultural and historical circumstances of their work actually impinge upon and constrain their classroom pedagogy - they are concerned about forms of resistance.

An alternative and more emancipatory possibility is to construe clinical supervision, with its emphasis on the practicalities and the here-and-now of teaching, as a path to self-understanding. By moving clinical supervision away from being a process exclusively associated with re-skilling teachers, to one that enables them to see their aspirations and express how they think and feel about teaching, then we begin to operate in ways that acknowledge the perplexities, dilemmas and contradictions that make teachers lives less than fulfilling. Even more than that, analyses of the kind being suggested become a way of teachers understanding themselves in their situation as products of certain social forces over which they can exercise increasing measures of control (Smyth, 1984c).

What this amounts to is adopting a 'critical' view not in terms of being negative, but rather a stance in which teachers are able to see their classroom actions in relation to the historical, social and cultural context in which they are embedded. This means using clinical supervision as a way in which teachers both individually and collectively can develop for themselves the capacity to view teaching historically; to treat the contemporary events, practices and structures of teaching problematically (and not take them for granted); and, to examine the surface realities of institutionalised schooling in a search for explanations of its forms, and thereby to clarify for themselves alternative courses of educational action that are open to them. Acting critically, therefore, refers to 'collaboration in marshalling intellectual capacity so as to focus upon analysing, reflecting on, and engaging in discourse about the nature and effects of practical aspects of teaching and how they might be altered' (Smyth, 1985d, p.9).

Apple (1975) summed it up when he said of the socially critical perspective:

> It requires a painful process of radically examining our current positions and asking pointed questions about the relationship that exists between these positions and the social structure from which they arise. It also necessitates a serious in-depth search for alternatives to these almost unconscious lenses we employ and the ability to cope with an ambiguous situation for which answers can now be only dimly seen and will not be easy to come by (p. 127).

He pointed out that the interests being served are those that relate to:

> ... the emancipation of individuals from lawlike rules and patterns of action ... so that they can reflect and act on the dialectical process of creating and

> recreating themselves and their institutions (p. 126).

Becoming critical and acting reflexively involves developing a realisation that 'persons are both the products and the creators of their own history' (Berlak & Berlak, 1981, p. 230). In practical terms this means teachers engaging themselves in systematic individual and social forms of investigation that examine the origins and consequences of everyday teaching behaviour so they come to see those factors that represent impediments to change. The intent is through collective action to overcome the fatalistic view that change in teaching is 'impossible for me', and seeing that circumstances can be different from what they are. It means moving from a 'passive ..., dependent, and adaptive' (Fay, 1977, p. 220) view of themselves and their potentialities, to one in which teachers are able to 'analyse and expose the hiatus between the actual and the possible, between the existing order of contradictions and a potential future state' (Held, 1980, p. 22). In short, it involves teachers becoming oriented to the development of an enhanced 'consciousness' of their own circumstances and a political involvement in working towards actively changing the frustrating and debilitating conditions that characterise their work lives.

An example (Smyth, 1985e) may serve to clarify the point. A maths teacher was concerned about possible side-effects of her individualised maths program. While she could see many advantages in working with students in ways that acknowledged the different pace at which they learn, she was uneasy about aspects of what she was doing. Certainly, the worksheets allowed students to pace their own learning, but she was concerned about the amount of time some students seemed to spend queuing up to see her about difficulties; she seemed to have a continuous line of students at her desk. Having a colleague collect evidence enabled her to confirm those feelings. Some students spent up to fifteen minutes in a lesson waiting to see the teacher. As she talked through the meaning of the data with her colleague, the issue became clearer. It was not so much a matter of solving a disabling problem by tinkering with her teaching to make it more efficient, so much as being able to see what was happening. Through the data they came to see how the curriculum form, in this case 'individualisation', dramatically influenced the nature of student-teacher relationships. The source of her unease was now evident - the teaching form and its attendant built-in pressure to deal with students in terse and impersonal ways. This was the reason for her feelings of frustration. In the short term, the consequence was that she was able to use ability grouping more so as to spend time interacting personally with students. The more important lesson, however, was that the teacher came to see clinical supervision as a way of transcending her teaching and penetrating its hidden assumptions about important pedagogical relationships.

Adopting a critical approach towards the use of clinical supervision is to do more than endorse a procedural orientation of a step-wise process aimed at describing and correcting problems within teaching. That approach may have utility under certain limited conditions, but there are larger issues. What is more important is a preparedness to reflect upon one's own history and how it is embedded in current practice, to speculate about the likely causes of relationships, but to also follow through into action whatever informed decisions to change that are deemed desirable. In developing this orientation, practitioners involved in clinical supervision need to address themselves to a number of fundamental questions about their teaching:

- how do our professional histories, individually and collectively, affect the way we teach?
- what are the taken-for-granted assumptions in our teaching?
- what are the theories of teaching we hold to be true?
- where do these theories come from?
- how do the ways we choose to teach lock us into certain kinds of relationships with our students?
- in what way does the structure of schooling determine our pedagogy, and how might we begin to change those structures?
- what are the unintended outcomes of our teaching?
- how can we create 'new' forms of

knowledge about teaching through discourse with colleagues?

Conclusion

I started out in this chapter with a plea to rescue clinical supervision from the current trend of viewing it as an instrumental and technocratic mode for the delivery of a service to certain categories of teachers perceived to be 'in need of the treatment'. Where it is used in this way, clinical supervision takes on all the hallmarks of an hierarchical administrative process used to cajole and coerce teachers into 'lifting their game'. What I suggest instead is a way of working with clinical supervision in which teachers themselves might begin to use it to uncover clinical knowledge about their own histories, teaching and institutional practices. Used in this way, I suggest that clinical supervision amounts to a way of investing teachers with more, rather than less control over their professional lives and destinies. The starting point was seen to lie in teachers problematising their teaching, as distinct from problem solving. By being able to render their teaching problematic, in the sense of using issues that perplex them as a way of getting behind the taken-for-granted habitualness of much of what they do, teachers are able to begin to see not only how their histories affect what they do, but how their forms of teaching and the institutional structures within which they work, constrain them. Being able to collectively reflect on the experiences and lessons gained while doing clinical supervision through establishing and extending dialogue among others similarly engaged, was suggested as a means by which schools can incorporate a constructively self-critical discussion into their ways of thinking and acting.

NOTES

Some of the notions contained in this chapter have been taken from a range of previous papers of mine without specific acknowledgement. The original ideas may be found in Smyth 1984b; 1985a; 1985b; 1985c; 1985d.

REFERENCES

Apple, M., Scientific interests and the nature of educational institutions, In W. Pinar (ed), Curriculum Theorizing, Berkeley : McCutchan, 1975

Beasley, B., The reflexive spectator in classroom research, INSET, 1 (2), 1981, 8-10

Benseman, J., Paulo Freire: a revolutionary alternative, Delta, 23, November 1978, 29-53

Berlak, A., Back to the basics: liberating pedagogy, Revised version of a paper presented to the annual meeting of the American Educational Research Association, Chicago, 1985

Berlak, A., & Berlak H., Dilemmas of Schooling: Teaching and Social Change, London: Methuen, 1981

Bernstein, R., The Restructuring of Social and Political Theory, London: Methuen, 1976

Chism, N., The place of peer interaction in teacher development: findings from a case study, Paper to the annual meeting of the American Educational Research Association, Chicago, 1985

Cogan, M., Clinical Supervision, Boston: Houghton -Mifflin, 1973

Curtis, D., Supervision of teachers: the Cogan cycle and its applicability to the Australian scene, In W. Mulford et al; Papers on A.C.T. Education 1974 5, Canberra: Canberra College of Advanced Education, 1975

Day, C., Teachers' thinking - intentions and practice: an action research perspective, In R. Halkes & J. Olson (eds) Teacher Thinking : A New Perspective on Persisting Problems in Education, Lisse: Swets & Zeitlinger, 1984

Devaney, K., Warmth, concreteness, time and thought in teachers' learning, In K. Devaney (ed), Essays on Teachers' Centers, San Francisco: Far West Laboratory for Educational Research and Development, 1977

Dewey, J., How We Think: A Restatement of the Relation of Reflective Thinking to the Educative Process, Chicago: Henry Regnevy, 1933

Doyle, W., Teaching as a profession: what we know and what we need to know about teaching, Austin, Texas: Research and Development Center for Teacher Education, University of

Texas at Austin, 1985

Elliott, J., Developing hypotheses about classrooms from teachers' practical constructs: an account of the Ford Teaching Project, *Interchange*, *7* (2), 1976, 2-22

Erickson, E., Verstehen and the method of disciplined subjectivity: the nature of clinical evidence, In L. Krimmerman (ed), *The Nature and Scope of Social Science: A Critical Anthology*, New York: Appleton-Century-Crofts, 1969, 721-35

Fay, B., How people change themselves: the relationship between critical theory and its audience, In T. Ball (ed), *Political Theory and Praxis : New Perspectives*, Minneapolis: University of Minnesota Press, 1977

Freedman, S. Jackson, J. & Boles, K., Teaching: an imperilled 'profession', In L. Shulman & G. Sykes (eds), *Handbook of Teaching and Policy*, New York : Longmans, 1983

Freidson, E., *Profession of Medicine: A Study of the Sociology of Applied Knowledge*, New York: David Mead, 1972

Fried, R., *Empowerment Versus Delivery of Services*, Concord, N.H: New Hampshire Department of Education, 1980

Goldhammer, R., *Clinical Supervision: Special Methods for the Supervision of Teachers*, New York: Holt, Rinehart & Winston, 1969

Goldhammer, R. Anderson, R. & Krajewski, R., *Clinical Supervision: Special Methods for the Supervision of Teachers*, (2nd ed), New York: Holt, Rinehart & Winston, 1980

Guditus, C., The pre-observation conference: is it worth the effort?, *Wingspan*, *1*, (1), 1982

Habermas, J., *Theory and Practice*, Boston: Beacon Press, 1973

Held, D., *An Introduction to Critical Theory: Horkheimer to Habermas*, London: Hutchinson, 1980

Hogben, D., The clinical mind: some implications for educational research and teacher training, *South Pacific Journal of Teacher Education*, *10*, (1), 1982

Holly, M., Teacher reflections on classroom life: collaboration and professional development, *The Australian Administrator*, *4*, (4), 1983. 1-4

Holly, M., *Keeping a Personal-Professional Journal*, Geelong, Australia: Deakin University Press, 1984

Jackson, P., Life in Classrooms, New York: Holt, Rinehart & Winston, 1968

Kilbourn, B., Linda: a case study of clinical supervision, Canadian Journal of Education, 7, (3), 1982, 1-24

Lortie, D., School Teacher: A Sociological Study, Chicago: University of Chicago Press, 1975

MacKay, D. & Marland P., Thought processes of teachers, Paper presented to the annual meeting of the American Educational Research Association, Toronto, 1978

Rudduck, J., Teaching as an art, teacher research and research-based teacher education, Second annual Lawrence Stenhouse Memorial Lecture, University of East Anglia, 1984

Ryan, W., Blaming the Victim, New York: Pantheon, 1971

Sergiovanni, T., Toward a theory of clinical supervision, Journal of Research and Development in Education, 9, (2), 1976, 20-29

Smyth, J., Clinical Supervision - Collaborative Learning About Teaching. A Handbook. Geelong, Australia: Deakin University Press, 1984a

Smyth, J., Teachers as collaborative learners in clinical supervision: a state-of-the-art review, Journal of Education for Teaching, 10, (1), 1984b, 24-38

Smyth, J., Toward a 'critical consciousness' in the instructional supervision of experienced teachers, Curriculum Inquiry, 14, (4), 1984c, 425-36

Smyth, J., Clinical supervision: technocratic mindedness, or emancipatory learning? Paper to the annual meeting of the South Pacific Association of Teacher Education, Hobart, Australia, 1985a

Smyth, J., An alternative and critical perspective for clinical supervision in schools, In K. Sirotnik & J. Oakes (eds), Critical Perspectives on the Organization and Improvement of Schooling, Massachussetts: Kluwer-Nijhoff, 1985b

Smyth, J., Changing what we do in our teaching: let's stop talking about it! Keynote address to a conference of Secondary Humanities Teachers, Lorne, Victoria, Australia, 1985c

Smyth, J., Developing a critical practice of clinical supervision, Journal of Curriculum Studies, 17, (1), 1985d, 1-15

Smyth, J., Becoming a reflective teacher, Deakin University: Unpublished manuscript, 1985e

Tripp, D., From autopilot to critical consciousness: problematising successful teaching, Revisions of a paper presented to the Sixth Curriculum Theory and Practice Conference Bergamo, Ohio, 1984. Unpublished manuscript, Murdoch Univeristy, Perth, Australia

Weller, R., An observational system for analysing clinical supervision of teachers, Unpublished doctoral dissertation, Harvard University, 1969

Withall, J. & Wood F., Taking the threat out of classroom observation and feedback, Journal of Teacher Education, 30, (1), 1979, 55-58

ACKNOWLEDGEMENT

Some of the ideas contained in this chapter have previously been published in the Journal of Education for Teaching and the Journal of Curriculum Studies. I am grateful for permission to republish those ideas here.

Chapter 5

CLINICAL SUPERVISION: TECHNICAL, COLLABORATIVE AND CRITICAL APPROACHES

John A. Retallick

In this chapter I propose to examine the literature on clinical supervision published since the beginning of the 1980's. Previous reviews (Reavis, 1978; Goldhammer, Anderson and Krajewski, 1980; Sullivan, 1980; Pavan, 1980) had assessed the state-of-the-art up until that time and set the scene for some advances in theory and research in the ensuing years. More recently a review by Pavan (1983) has considered much of the unpublished dissertation research, so this review will be largely confined to published sources.

One of the characteristics of the earlier reviews was a generally unreflective and uncritical approach to the epistemological basis of the research under review. In part at least, this could probably be attributed to the relatively restricted range of research methods being employed by researchers into clinical supervision at that time. However, theory, research and practice have diversified considerably in the past five years and there now appears to be a need for systematic attention to some of the assumptions which underpin the various approaches. Snyder (1981) pointed to the emerging diversity:

> Perceptions in the 1980's about the skill needs of teachers could shape clinical supervision into little more than a refined teacher inspection technology ... Clinical supervision could emerge less as an evaluation tool and more as a coaching system (p. 521).

In carrying out this review I shall attempt to identify a number of distinctly different understandings of clinical supervision and interrelated methodologies for researching the process. These various approaches will be located within a contemporary epistemological framework drawn from Habermas (1971) and Fay (1975), which should serve to illuminate their underlying assumptions.

Conflicting Assumptions Underlying Educational Research

Popkewitz (1984) has recently drawn our attention to the existence of three competing intellectual traditions in social and educational research in the western world. He refers to the empirical-analytic sciences, of which the behavioural sciences form the largest and most powerful segment; symbolic or linguistic sciences; and critical sciences. Each of these traditions contains different assumptions about the social world, different purposes and methods of research, and different views about the role of the researcher in educational inquiry.

The realisation of the existence of these competing traditions is important in approaching the task of a review of literature because very often the assumptions underlying a particular viewpoint or research study are not made explicit:

> the power of the underlying assumptions in science is that they do not appear as such but are contained in the different customs, conventions and findings of research (Popkewitz, 1984 : 35).

In seeking out the roots of the three traditions and their conflicting assumptions I turn to Habermas (1971) who has shown how the production of knowledge through the sciences is guided by fundamental knowledge-constitutive interests of humankind. Three forms of science have been created to give definition and structure to research activities which pursue knowledge in connection with those interests:

- the empirical-analytic sciences seek formal, law like explanations of natural or physical phenomena and incorporate a technical interest in prediction and control of those phenomena;
- the historical-hermeneutic (or interpretive) sciences seek understanding of meaning in the human or cultural realm through interpretation of

communicative actions and incorporate a practical interest in enhancing communication;
. the critical sciences go beyond an interpretive understanding to a reconstruction of events and the uncovering of personal repressions and structural constraints which serve to maintain and legitimate forms of domination in social relationships which can in principle be transformed, thereby incorporating an emancipatory interest.

The existence of these three sciences in the field of supervision and evaluation has previously been pointed out by Sergiovanni (1982) who also claims that 'mainstream thought continues its quest to develop a science or technology of classroom supervision embedded in the measurement and evaluation disciplines' (p. 1).

In the literature on clinical supervision it is evident that some writers are seeking to embed the process into that mainstream thinking whilst others are developing it as a genuinely alternative form of professional development; that is to say, as a practice of professional development for educators in its own right. For evidence of the former trend we can turn to the empirical-analytic research studies and the associated technical-behavioural science approach to the practice of clinical supervision.

The Behavioural Science Model

Empirical-analytic research on teaching and clinical supervision fuels the quest for a behavioural science of supervision. The research is typically conducted on assumptions and with procedures that were developed for research in the natural sciences. This is usually known as the positivist tradition which, amongst other things, assumes that there are context-free, universal laws of teaching and supervising waiting to be discovered. The experimental research design and the statistical analysis of data are assumed to be the correct scientific procedures since it is also assumed that there is a methodological unity in the sciences; that there is only one proper scientific method. The experimental paradigm also serves as the ideal model for various types of non-experimental research, such as sample surveys and field studies in schools where variables are isolated and manipulated. The procedures are aimed at removing the variables from personal and social contexts which are sometimes regarded as contaminants of the data.

The possibility that this approach might be inappropriate to the social sciences is the subject of a long and rich debate (see note 1) but for the moment we need to look at the impact of positivism on the research and practice of clinical supervision. Two examples of recent research studies may serve to illustrate the approach.

In the first, Isherwood (1983) sought to discover if three variables (verbal behaviour of principal; the basis of authority the principal had over teachers; and the frequency of clinical supervision behaviour) were statistically related to the perceptions of effective clinical supervision. The method was to ask principals for their perceptions of these relationships in a university-based workshop situation. The only conclusion to emerge was that principals thought that indirect verbal behaviour was more effective.

The major inadequacy of approaches like this to research is that they fail to advance our knowledge of clinical supervision in the real world. Since the research process is isolated from the schools where clinical supervision actually happens and occurs in a laboratory-type setting in the university, there can be no real enlightenment. Because the research variables, methods and findings are construed as context-free they have little meaning.

A second study which exemplifies the positivist tradition is reported by Grimmett and Housego (1983). This study differs from the first in that it investigated clinical supervision in a naturalistic setting where four volunteer supervisors and teachers participated in two cyles of clinical supervision. Conference dialogue was recorded and replayed for stimulated recall of thought processes and the collected data were analysed particularly for a variable identified as 'supervisor's level of conceptual functioning'. The authors claimed that for effective implementation of clinical supervision only supervisors who are capable of functioning at a high conceptual level should be utilized, and they assert that such a limitation would reduce the amount of clinical supervision practiced because there are few supervisors who would meet the minimum conceptual level requirement.

There are numerous problems of a different

kind with this research. Though the study was carried out in a naturalistic setting there is still an attempt made by the researchers to isolate particular variables in a way which lifts clinical supervision out of the social and historical context in which it actually occurred. Furthermore, the search for psychological variables located in individual research subjects is a reductionist view (see note 2) which has limited potential for increasing our understanding of what is essentially a social process. Clinical supervision, as a social process, is constituted through communicative actions and it must be viewed holistically to understand how it is socially constructed and maintained. Additionally, there is little to be gained from following a line of research which has the effect of restricting the utilization of clinical supervision to a select few - the more widely it is adopted amongst teachers the greater the chance of understanding its strengths and weaknesses.

These two research studies illustrate the empirical-analytic or positivist approach which seeks to identify context-free variables and generate law like generalisations. The implementation of the findings from this type of research activity is usually in the form of the application of technique or technology. Indeed, there seems to be a quite widely held view that clinical supervision is a technique or technology for putting into place certain prescribed approaches to teaching and learning drawn from the behavioural science research.

The Technical Approach to Clinical Supervision

The recent literature provides some clear examples of what might be called a technical approach to clinical supervision. Emphasis is placed on the application of techniques for increased control and predictability in the teaching-learning situation. From this point of view it can be seen as a 'delivery system' for ensuring conformity to a particular teaching approach in the classroom.

In the Hunter model (Hunter 1984; 1985) for example, teaching is regarded as 'an applied science derived from research in human learning and human behavior' (1984, p.171) and it is claimed that 'translation of research-based theory into practice, has now been accomplished' (1984, p.174). The foundation of the model is behaviourist learning theory which addresses the question: 'Does observable behavior validate that learning has occurred?' (1984, p.175). Associated with that is a reinforcement model of teaching : 'Is the teacher regularly reinforcing productive new behaviour when it emerges, but changing to an intermittent schedule of reinforcement for productive behavior that is not new?' (1984, p.175). The model is completed with a version of clinical supervision that aims to coach teachers to put into place the prescribed view of teaching and learning: 'the observer must be familiar with those principles of learning, recognize them in action, and determine, on the basis of objective evidence, whether they are being used appropriately, being ignored or being abused' (1984, p.179).

Though this is not the place for a critique of behaviourist learning theory (see note 3) I have some concerns about the use of clinical supervision in a behaviourist model of teaching and learning. The behaviourists argue, as does Hunter (1985, p.59), that their concept of learning is universal, that is it applies without exception to all human beings in all learning situations. It therefore excludes any other form of knowledge about learning and in so doing it arbitrarily limits our conception of knowledge. The use of clinical supervision in line with this view can only be as a technology for imposing and refining teaching practices which are consistent with a behaviourist view of learning. In the case of the Hunter model the technology is in the form of a number of 'templates' for describing, interpreting and evaluating aspects of teaching internally consistent with the model.

Since in the supervision process 'the primary responsibility for analysing possible causality and suggesting remediation rests with the observer' (Hunter, 1984, p.181) it is clear that the teacher is well and truly 'trapped' within the predetermined model. Clinical supervision is conceptualised as an unproblematic technology of control in the behavioural science model. This makes it a profoundly conservative process since it does not seek to generate forms of consciousness which could enable teachers to question the model or strive towards alternative possibilities.

A second example of a technical approach to

clinical supervision can be seen in the work of Acheson and Gall (1980). What makes this one a technical approach is not simply the emphasis on techniques in clinical supervision (which are necessary for anyone to be competent) but rather it is because that is all there is to their model. Acheson and Gall acknowledge their debt to the pioneers of the field - Goldhammer (1969) and Cogan (1973) and then proceed to reduce the process from what they envisaged to a mere set of techniques. The extent of the reduction can be seen in Table 5.1

TABLE 5.1

The Process of Clinical Supervision

Goldhammer's Stages	Cogan's Phases	Acheson & Gall's Phases
1. Preobservation conference	1. Establishing the supervisor relationships	1. Planning conference
2. Observation	2. Planning with the teacher	2. Observation
3. Analysis and Strategy	3. Planning the strategy of the observation	3. Feedback conference
4. Supervisory conference	4. Observing instruction	
5. Post-conference analysis	5. Analysing the teaching-learning process	
	6. Planning the strategy of the conference	
	7. Conference	
	8. Renewed Planning	

Source: Pavan, 1980, p.248

It is not only the reduction in number of steps that is noticeable in Table 5.1, but what is important is the nature of the revision to the process that occurs when Goldhammer's stage 5 is omitted. Post-conference analysis was, for Goldhammer, an integral and vital part of the process which enables the supervisor to maintain the stance of a reflexive participant in the process. The post-conference analysis was designed as a kind of postmortem or professional self- examination wherein the supervisor would have his or her work subjected to a rigorous analysis similar to the analysis of the teacher's work:

> If what's good for the goose is inadequate for the gander, in this field, then something is the matter, for it is all but impossible to imagine a rational double standard that could free supervisors from the necessity of being supervised themselves (Goldhammer, 1969, p.273).

In the post-conference analysis the supervisor can carefully and systematically reflect on his or her own supervision. That is to say the supervisor himself or herself becomes an object of analysis; without this the supervisor has only one objective of analysis in mind, and that is the teacher. It is necessary to recover the idea of post-conference analysis, abandoned by Acheson and Gall (1980), if clinical supervision is to be more than a set of techniques unilaterally applied by supervisor to teacher.

A technical view of clinical supervision has also been put forward by Krajewski (1982). He has stated seven concepts upon which he believes all clinical supervision programs must be constructed:

> 1. Deliberate intervention into the instructional process;
> 2. Creates productive tensions for both teacher and supervisor, which;
> 3. Requires supervisor knowledge and training. Clinical supervision thus;
> 4. Is a technology for improving instruction, which;
> 5. Is goal oriented, systematic, yet flexible, and;
> 6. Requires mutual trust and support nurturance. It also;

7. Fosters role delineation (Krajewski, 1982, p. 41-42)

Again it is the unilateral view implicit here that is disturbing. Viewed in this way clinical supervision is a technology made up of knowledge, skills and techniques which can be acquired by supervisors and applied to teachers in much the way that a piece of technological equipment might be used. For many, no doubt, this is a reassuring view. It is reassuring because it enables supervisors to think of clinical supervision as a means by which they might keep a step ahead and above teachers. I would submit that this is an erroneous view. Clearly there is a need for an alternative way of understanding clinical supervision.

The Interpretive Approach to Social Science

One alternative to the behavioural science model and empirical-analytic research methods is to be found in interpretive social science. This tradition of inquiry finds expression in such approaches as phenomenology, hermeneutics and ethnography which seek to replace the notions of law like explanation, predictions and control with the interpretive notions of understanding, meaning and intention. There is an underlying assumption that human behaviour is rule-governed social action and is thereby clearly distinguished from the natural or physical world. It is argued that the unique quality of being human is in our ability to invent symbols which communicate meaning and therefore a research method appropriate to the social sciences should be sensitive to that quality.

As Fay (1975) points out, to understand social action requires more than mere observation of physical behaviour; it requires an interpretation on the part of the observer because any action concept involves reference to either the subject's intentions, plans or desires, or, moral, legal or social rules in accordance with which the subject is acting. An interpretive social science seeks to describe actions in such a way as to make clear these elements of the action, which is to say that it tries to reveal the meaning of the action from the actor's point of view.

The outcome of the research process is a practical one; it is to increase the possibilities for mutual understanding, mutual influence and communication between groups and individuals who are involved in it or come into contact with accounts of it. Such an outcome is said to be possible because an interpretive understanding reveals what it is like to be in the position of the other person or group; it is entering their 'world' or their culture to see things from their perspective. In so doing it not only increases the possibility of communication but it helps to unravel distortions of communication which might have existed due to misunderstandings about what it is like to be in another person's situation.

McCutcheon (1981) has examined the nature of the interpretive endeavour in classroom observations. She sees interpretation 'as a transaction between the researcher's knowledge and the observations being made and (it) therefore places a researcher in an active role in the construction of meaning' (pp. 9-10). It reveals both the subject (the researcher) and the object (phenomenon under study). This is very different from the objectivist assumption of positivist research and it can be anticipated that this approach will involve quite different research methods and incorporate a more holistic view of clinical supervision as a professional practice.

The Collaborative Practice of Clinical Supervision

Garman (1982) has raised our understanding of clinical supervision from the level of technique to a collaborative professional practice and has thereby extended the line of thinking of the originators - Cogan and Goldhammer. As she says:

> clinical supervision as a concept is different from the procedural orientation popularly described in the literature. In other words the classic eight phase process known as 'the cycle of supervison' is useful under limited conditions, but does not define the practice itself (p. 35).

The concepts of colleagiality, collaboration, skilled service and ethical conduct stake out the domain of the clinical approach to supervision according to Garman's interpretation. The concepts define the frame of mind of the clinical supervisor, the nature of educational alliances or involvements entered into by supervisor and teacher, the inquiry skills of clinical supervision, and the standards of behaviour required of professional practice.

Garman emphasises the significance of language development and communication as the basis upon which the practice of clinical supervision rests. The negotiation of agreements is a key feature. There is freedom from predetermined systems of teaching as supervisor and teacher together search for fresh and deeper perspectives on their work. The inquiry skills of discovery, verification, explanation, interpretation and evaluation were revealed in The Mousetrap Study (Garman, 1982, pp.50-51), a five year study at the University of Pittsburgh, as being necessary modes of inquiry in supervisory practice (see note 4).

Also revealed in The Mousetrap Study was the importance of stable data in clinical supervision practice. Over the years of the study some 300 supervisors were shown a film of a classroom lesson and asked to identify the teacher's intent for the lesson and the extent to which she achieved her intent. First they were asked to use their own observation notes of the lesson and make a response; later they were given copies of a verbatim transcript of the lesson as an example of clinical data and asked to make a second response. A large discrepancy between the two responses showed the clinical data to provide a far more accurate or stable data base. Detailed results of this study can be found in Garman (1985).

Another strand of The Mousetrap Study led to a hermeneutic study (see note 5) of educational myth in the practice of clinical supervision (Holland, 1983). An educational myth is seen as an emotional expression through language and ritual of sacred truths about educational experience, unconscious in nature and often evoked for the purpose of prescribing thought and action about education. The procedures of the study involved distinguishing and interpreting elements of myth in writings about educational experiences generated by supervisors. An understanding of the existence and nature of myths about education is useful in clinical supervision practice.

A study by Kilbourn (1982) adds a further dimension to our understanding of the essence of a collaborative practice of clinical supervision.

He desribes three features that he regards as vital to the spirit of clinical supervision : there is respect for the teacher's autonomy in a colleagial relationship, evidence from actual teaching of repeated patterns relating to teacher's intentions and student consequences is the basis of action by supervisor and teacher, and, particular events in the process are viewed in terms of historical and contextual continuity. Utilising a case study research method himself and commenting on methodology Kilbourn suggests that:

> articulating (the) features and detecting them in practice will depend largely on the wisdom gained from studying specific cases of clinical supervision since it is in specific instances of clinical supervision, complete with historical background, that give life and meaning to the practice (1982, p.2).

Other case study research has also shed some light on what actually happens in clinical supervision encounters. Robinson's (1984) account of how he introduced clinical supervision to a colleague in his school, had as its focus the nature of change. The study reveals the importance of the teacher as the initiator of desired change for there to be deep and lasting commitment, though a sensitive supervisor can be a stimulus for the teacher to initiate change. It also reveals that the teacher's self-image is at stake both in the clinical supervision relationship and in connection with changes that might be occurring in classroom procedures.

From the other side of the clinical supervision relationship McCoombe (1981) provides an account of the teacher's perspective which, as he notes, is sadly lacking in the literature in comparison with the supervisor's perspective or that of the outside researcher. McCoombe reveals a number of concerns of the teacher at the beginning of the cycle - the time involved, the 'invasion' of his classroom by other personnel, the reactions of the children to their teacher being observed, the ability of the supervisor to accurately collect data and, perhaps most importantly from his point of view, the possible exposure of his faults as a teacher. This is a salutary reminder that it is hallowed ground upon which the clinical supervisor treads.

Peer Clinical Supervision

note

The problematic nature of the difference in status between supervisors and teachers in a hierarchical structure has led to the development of peer clinical supervision. In one of the pioneering studies in this development Goldsberry (1980) had this to say:

> Perhaps the status difference between supervisors and teachers drastically inhibits the development of collegial dialogue. This gulf would seem especially likely when the supervisor is also charged with the formal evaluation of the teacher, as is typically the case in elementary schools where the building principal is the sole administrative officer (p. 12).

In order to make a distinction between clinical supervision which incorporates a supervisor - teacher status differential and an interaction for mutual benefit between peers, Goldsberry named the latter process 'colleague consultation'. He sees its as entirely consistent with the original (Cogan and Goldhammer) version of clinical supervision:

> Since the clinical supervision model is constructed around a premise of colleagial relations between participants, the application of this model in a peer collaboration context seems entirely congruent with its philosophical base (1980 p.14).

The 'colleague consultation' interpretation of the clinical supervision process is based upon five assumptions:

1. Professional development is an ongoing function for teachers;
2. Given a method and an opportunity which is non-threatening, relevant, and rewarding, teachers will analyse and where possible, improve their teaching;
3. Feedback from knowledgeable observers regarding classroom events offers

teachers an expanded perceptual base;

4. The delivery of feedback from classroom observers can either inhibit teachers or encourage teachers to reflect upon and alter their own teaching behaviours;
5. Advantages are realized when classroom teachers, rather than supervisory personnel, observe and confer with their teaching colleagues (1980, p.42).

In a later report incorporating aspects of the 1980 study, Alfonso and Goldsberry (1982) list a number of advantages of colleague consultation. First, it mobilises the human resources of a school in a joint effort to improve instruction. Second, it can produce a sense of personal achievement for teachers as well as a better functioning school. Third, it is likely to encourage the introduction of instructional innovations. However, in seeking to place it in a social context they also point out that there are organisational barriers in schools which impede the development of colleague consultation and therefore transformations are needed: 'A call for colleagueship in supervision is also a call, then, for new organizational forms and patterns of interaction in schools' (1982 p.103).

Another study which sought to investigate peer clinical supervision in context is reported by McFaul (1982) and McFaul and Cooper (1984). This case study of the implementation of the process in one school focussed on:

1. the variations or configurations of the process as implemented by teachers,
2. the contextual or environmental factors within the school setting and their congruence with the peer clinical supervision model, and
3. the feasibility of the model for elementary teachers' use.

Participants in the study, twelve elementary teachers, undertook a one semester course in clinical supervision of which the final four weeks entailed the conduct of four cycles with other participants. Data consisted of the documentation of the cycles, ethnographic fieldnotes and self-reports in various forms including interviews, reaction sheets and written responses to questions. The documentation data revealed that there were variations in the way teachers implemented the process though 'always honoring what might be called a 'gentlewoman's agreement' that no one would be made uncomfortable in the process' (1982, p.121).

The ethnographic data were interpreted in terms of four themes - isolation and fragmentation, stratification, standardisation and reactionism. These themes described the contextual features of the school setting. Teachers were isolated from each other because of the architecture of the school and there were tensions between various groups of staff which the peer clinical supervision process did not appear to overcome. The stratification theme described the way teachers and pupils in the school experienced hierarchically assigned reward systems stemming mainly from the principal and this appeared to add to the isolation and fragmentation of staff; stratification discouraged teachers from perceiving each other as equals. Standardisation or sameness of teaching procedure, mainly imposed by administration or textbooks, was evident and there seemed little room for individualism. The reactionism theme related to the question of teacher initiative or teacher reaction in professional decision making; it appeared that teachers could do little else but react in a situation were they had little sense of power in decision making.

These findings are summed up in relation to peer clinical supervision:

> All of these factors seemed innately incongruent with the peer clinical supervision model which emphasised a need for colleagiality and trust, not isolation and fragmentation; which expected peers to meet and work with each other as equals and not in terms of a stratified hierarchy; which encouraged teachers to search out their own personal teaching patterns and styles rather than perfect standardised models; and which called for a sense of professional initiative and decision-making rather than a reactive, uncertain stance (McFaul, 1982, pp.136-37).

McFaul (1982) and McFaul and Cooper (1984)

conclude that the form and spirit of peer clinical supervision is out of touch with the reality of life in schools. Their critics, Goldsberry (1984) and Krajewski (1984) claim that the design and delivery of the intervention, that is, the actual implementation of the process, may have been seriously flawed and it may never have had a reasonable chance.

Studying Implementation Processes

Studies by Smyth, Henry and Martin (1982) and Smyth, et. al., (1982) on the implementation of clinical supervision could shed some light on the above controversy. In the first of those two studies, the authors report an attempt to introduce clinical supervision to three schools. The collection of data was by participant-observation procedures. The study focussed on:

1. whether teachers and supervisors could be assisted to develop positive attitudes towards clinical supervision;
2. whether teachers perceive clinical supervision to be a valuable form of inservice professional development; and
3. whether the practices as actually implemented in some case study schools were an accurate interpretation of the clinical model.

Information on clinical supervision was provided to participants in a one day workshop and throughout the school term by consultants from the university who also observed and gathered data. The approach taken by the consultants was significant:

> the researchers adopted a conscious policy of allowing school participants to accept full 'ownership' of the activity. There was a deliberate attempt made to work with school personnel rather than for or on them (Smyth, Henry and Martin, 1982, p.2).

The data reveal that the implementation process was successful in two out of three schools. The lack of success in one school was attributed to crossed and confused lines of communication which resulted in teachers feeling that they had been excluded from participation in some early implementation decisions; they became hostile and negative towards the innovation. Rapport amongst staff was regarded as critical to successful implementation as were the personal qualities, knowledge and skills of the supervisor. Also found to be important was the background information supplied to participants:

> Steps should be taken to ensure that volunteer participants understand the teacher-centred nature of clinical supervision, the kinds of personal relationships required in enacting the clinical supervision process, the demands that will be made on their time, and the sustained long-term nature of the effort required in ongoing professional development (Smyth, Henry and Martin, 1982, p.4).

In the second study Smyth, et. al., (1982) reflected on their earlier endeavours and found some shortcomings:

> While we were impressed with the robustness of the clinical model and the way teachers were prepared to embrace it as an alternative mode of inservice education, we were less than satisfied with our own methods of operating with and helping teachers use the process (p.8).

In other words this group of researchers turned the 'blowtorch' on themselves and their ways of collaborating with teachers to introduce clinical supervision to schools (see note 6). As a result of deliberating on their experiences they developed a new way of implementing clinical supervision which they called the 'follow-through model'; see figure 5.1

FIGURE 5.1
The Follow-through Model

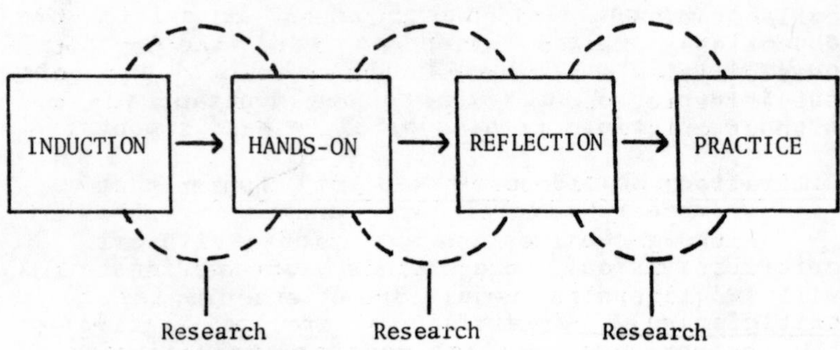

Source : Smyth, et. al., 1982, p.18

The model recognises some important features of an implementation process:

a. change is incremental and developmental;
b. real change occurs slowly;
c. lasting change occurs only as a consequence of teachers endorsing proposed changes as being practical and having intrinsic merit;
d. teachers need opportunity to talk through the implications of any new strategy with their colleagues;
e. teachers need to be able to see that problems they are experiencing may be common to other teachers;
f. it enables mutual support to be given both before and after hands-on experience with clinical supervision:

A number of understandings about the follow-through model were generated in the research study. It was learnt that it is a powerful means of converting ideas into action - providing for actual trials of new ideas overcomes many aspects of the personal and social inertia to change. The provision of on-site assistance is helpful for teachers and also exposes where change is cosmetic. People with different kinds of expertise can collaborate together provided that co-operation is accepted as the key to successful collaboration.

The interpretive research methods and the associated conception of clinical supervision as a collaborative practice outlined in this section represent a clear alternative to the behavioural-technical model outlined earlier. The collaborative approach overcomes many of the objections raised earlier and extends the possibilities of clinical supervision. However, the interpretive approach to social science is not without critics.

Limitations of Interpretive Social Science

Although there are a number of lines of criticism of the interpretive approach just two will be mentioned here. The first relates to a criticism that since the approach is limited to the uncovering of actors' meanings and definitions of the situation in which they are involved it cannot penetrate the social conditions which have given rise to those meanings and definitions. Interpretive explanations cannot legitimately go beyond the actors' immediate understandings. The origins and causes of those understandings and the links with social reality and circumstances beyond the actors' perceptions are left unexplained. Largely because of this, interpretive explanations neglect the crucial problems of social conflict and social change.

A second source of criticism is of the relationship between theory and practice in interpretive social science. It is claimed that the clarification of meanings that people hold of their situation will open up the possibilities for communication and through that people will reinterpret their situation and change their actions. However, this ignores the fact that most people experience some form of resistance to alternative interpretations of what they are doing. New interpretations are more likely to be seen as emotional threats and therefore discarded or at least strongly resisted. These and other limitations of interpretive social science have provided the stimulus for a criticial approach.

An Emerging Critical Perspective

Sergiovanni (1982) has suggested that we are at a watershed in the development of thought about supervision of teaching. Whilst in the broader field of supervision the behavioural science view may prevail it is the interpretive-collaborative approach to clinical supervision which has established the process as a genuine alternative.

Complementing and extending the collaborative approach is an emerging critical perspective, drawn largely from the Frankfurt School tradition (see note 7) which has the potential to take our theory, research and practice in new directions.

The critical approach takes as its starting point the interpretive-collaborative notion of clinical supervision and seeks to overcome some of the limitations of that approach. As Smyth (1984a) suggests, a critical practice of clinical supervision 'has to do with colleagues who have been working collaboratively together carrying their collaboration a stage further' (p. 45). He sees this being actualised by teacher and colleague-observer reflecting critically on the efficacy of the process in the post-conference analysis.

It has been argued by Smyth (1984b) that the beginnings of a critical perspective on clinical supervision can be found in the works of Cogan (1973) and Goldhammer (1969). Certainly the former was unequivocal about the importance of non-hierarchical or collaborative relationships:

> clinical supervision is conceptualized as the interaction of peers and colleagues. It is not unilateral action taken by the supervisor and aimed at the teacher (Cogan, 1973,p.xi).

It was Goldhammer's (1969) idea of the supervisor actually reflecting upon the experience of clinical supervision in the post-conference analysis that gave his work a critical edge to it. Goldhammer's own method of post-conference analysis was to tape-record supervision conferences and replay them a number of times:

> As I listen the second time (or third), I pay special attention to Teacher's words and inflections and try very hard to discipline myself from projecting feelings upon him. I try, in other words, to break free from my own feelings - for example, that at some particular moment I had been particularly supportive or accepting or instructive or punitive - and listen to Teacher's responses to see what clues they provide about how teacher was

> actually responding to my behavior, or feeling about things generally. Even after this kind of effort, possibilities of self-deception remain, but at least one has tried to see things as realistically as possible (p. 275) (my emphasis).

It is that 'possibility of self-deception' that justifies and makes necessary a critical element in the practice of clinical supervision. Without systematic reflection on their actual dialogue with teachers, supervisors will neither be aware of nor able to correct deceptions and distortions in their practice. Of particular importance are deceptions and distortions generated by the exercise of power in hierarchical supervisor-teacher relationships. Again, as Goldhammer pointed out:

> I am especially enthusiastic about the idea of having the teacher who is being supervised fill the role of Supervisor's supervisor at propitious moments ... I am becoming progressively more convinced that one measure to relieve some of the old status anxieties of supervision, to cut across its real and imagined hierarchies, to enhance Teacher's feeling of dignity in the supervisory relationship, to enable Teacher to gain higher degrees of objective distance in his own work, and to keep supervisor fully aware of the taste of his own medicine, is to create precisely such role-reversals on a regular and dependable basis (p. 279).

For Smyth (1984a) the way towards a critical practice for clinical supervision is through a reconstruction of Goldhammer's fifth stage, in critical terms. This could mean supervisor and teacher together subjecting their practice to questions like:

- whose interests are being served?
- who exercises control?
- what is feasible and possible, in the circumstances?
- what are the likely results or effects? (p.47).

Or, questions such as :

- to what extent are the practices of clinical supervision just in treating teachers as rational and capable of participating fully in the determination of their own destiny?
- to what extent is the process of clinical supervision practical in allowing teachers to discover aspects about their own teaching through actions?
- to what extent is clinical supervision realistic in acknowledging the facts of school and classroom life? (p.47).

Smyth (1984c) has viewed clinical supervision as a process that enables teachers to exercise a measure of empowerment over their own teaching. Through using the process to gain insights and acquire understandings of their teaching, to analyse and theorise about their teaching, to reflect on the social antecedents and possible consequences of their teaching it is argued that teachers are engaging in a form of critical inquiry which is professionally liberating.

Finally, for my own part I find the concept of symmetrical communication or the 'ideal speech situation' within the theory of communicative action (Habermas, 1979, p. 1984) to be a key construct in a critical method of clinical supervision. Clearly, clinical supervision is constituted through communication between the participants. A functional analysis of the dialogue roles used to constitute the process reveals a depth understanding of the nature of the collaborative relationship. Given a systematic way of analysing their own conference transcripts along these lines participants are able to reflect upon their own communication processes and seek ways of overcoming the asymmetries which are typical of supervisory structures in schools. There is considerable potential in the insights of critical theory for providing new understandings and new possibilities for the practice of clinical supervision.

NOTES

1. For example T. Adorno, et. al., The Positivist Dispute in German Sociology,

Heinemann, London, 1976; R. J. Bernstein, The Restructuring of Social and Political Theory, University of Pennsylvania Press, Pennsylvania, 1978; and B. Fay, Social Theory and Political Practice, George Allen and Unwin, London, 1975.

2. 'Reductionism holds that to understand the world requires disassembling it into its component parts, and that these parts are in some way more fundamental than the wholes they compose ...' (S. Rose, The Limits to Science, Science for the People, 16, (6), 1984, p.25).

3. This has been accomplished elsewhere. See for example W. Feinberg, Understanding Education : Toward a Reconstruction of Educational Inquiry, Cambridge University Press, Cambridge, 1983.

4. I am indebted to Dr. Noreen Garman for providing me with information on this study during her visit to Australia in September 1983.

5. A useful introduction to hermeneutics is provided in Z. Bauman, Hermeneutics and Social Science, Hutchison, London, 1978. Briefly, it refers to methods of recovering and understanding the true meaning of written texts or documents.

6. Dr. John Smyth pointed this out to me during a personal conversation in September 1985.

7. The Frankfurt School of critical theory is a tradition of philosophy and research which originated in the Institute of Social Research established in Frankfurt in 1923 and is continued in the work of Jurgen Habermas who is currently Professor of Philosophy at the University of Frankfurt. An overview of tradition can be found in M. Jay, The Dialectical Imagination, Little, Brown & Co., Boston, 1973; or D. Held, An Introduction to Critical Theory, Hutchison, London, 1980. An account of Habermas' critical theory can be found in T. McCarthy, The Critical Theory of Jurgen Habermas, MIT Press, Cambridge Mass., 1978.

REFERENCES

Acheson, K. & Gall, M., Techniques in the Clinical Supervision of Teaching: Preservice and Inservice Applications, New York, Longman,

1980

Alfonso, R. & Goldsberry, L., Colleagueship in Supervision. In T. Sergiovanni (ed) Supervision of Teaching, Alexandria, Va: Association for Supervision and Curriculum Development, 1982

Cogan, M., Clinical Supervision, Boston: Houghton Mifflin, 1973

Fay, B., Social Theory and Political Practice, London: George Allen & Unwin, 1975

Garman, N., The clinical approach to supervision, In T. Sergiovanni (ed) Supervision of Teaching, Alexandria, Va: Association for Supervision and Curriculum Development, 1982

Garman, N., Clinical supervision: quackery or remedy for professional development, Journal of Supervision and Curriculum, 1985, (in press)

Goldhammer, R., Clinical Supervision: Special Methods for the Supervision of Teachers, New York : Holt Rinehart & Winston, 1969

Goldhammer, R., Anderson, R., and Krajewski, R., Clinical Supervision: Special Methods for the Supervision of Teachers, 2nd ed. New York: Holt Rinehart & Winston, 1980

Goldsberry, L., Colleague consultation: teacher collaboration using a clinical supervision model, Unpublished doctoral dissertation, University of Illinois at Urbana - Champaign, 1980

Goldsberry, L., Reality - really? A response to McFaul and Cooper, Educational Leadership, 41, (7,) 1984, 10-11

Grimmett, P & Housego, I., Interpersonal relationships in the clinical supervision conference, The Canadian Administrator, 22, 1983

Habermas, J., Knowledge and Human Interests, Boston: Beacon, 1971

Habermas, J., Communication and the Evolution of Society, Boston: Beacon, 1979

Habermas, J., The Theory of Communicative Action, Vol. l. Boston: Beacon, 1984

Holland, P., A hermeneutic study of educational myth: implications for clinical supervision, Unpublished doctoral dissertation, University of Pittsburgh, 1983.

Hunter, M., Knowing, teaching and supervising, In Hosford, P. (ed), Using What We Know About Teaching, Alexandria, Va: Association for Supervision and Curriculum Development, 1984

Hunter, M., What's wrong with Madeline Hunter?, Educational Leadership, 42, (5) 1985, 7-60

Isherwood, G., Clinical supervision: a principal's perspective, Journal of Educational Administration, 21, (1), 1983, 14-20

Kilbourn, B., Linda: a case study in clinical supervision, Canadian Journal of Education, 7, (3), 1982, 1-24

Krajewski, R., Clinical supervision: a conceptual framework, Journal of Research and Development in Education, 15, (2), 1982, 38-43

Krajewski, R., No wonder it didn't work: a response to McFaul and Cooper, Educational Leadership, 41, (7), 1984, 11

McCoombe, M., Clinical supervision from the inside, Australian Administrator Research Monograph, No. 1, 1981, 1-22

McCutcheon, G., On the interpretation of classroom observations, Educational Researcher, 10, (5), 1981, 5-10

McFaul, S. A case study of the implementation of peer clinical supervision in an urban elementary school, Unpublished doctoral dissertation, University of Houston, 1982

McFaul, S. & Cooper, J., Peer clinical supervision: theory vs reality, Educational Leadership, 4, (7), 1984, 5-9

Pavan, B., Clinical supervision: some signs of progress, Texas Tech Journal of Education, 7, (3), 1980, 241-251

Pavan, B., Clinical supervision: does it make a difference, Paper presented at Annual Meeting of the Council of Professors of Instructional Supervision, November 1983; ERIC Document Service ED 242094

Popkewitz, T., Paradigm and Ideology in Educational Research, Lewes: Falmer, 1984

Reavis, C., Clinical supervision: a review of the research, Educational Leadership, 35, (7), 1978, 580-84

Robinson, G., A second pair of eyes: a case study of a supervisor's view of clinical supervision, In J. Smyth (ed), Case Studies in Clinical Supervision, Geelong: Deakin University Press, 1984, 3-42

Sergiovanni, T., Supervision and evaluation: interpretive and critical perspectives, Paper presented at the Annual Meeting of the Council of Professors of Instructional Supervision, November 12, 1982

Smyth, J., Henry, C., and Martin, J., Clinical

supervision: evidence of a viable strategy for teacher development, The Australian Administrator, 3, (5), 1982, 1-4

Smyth, J., et. al., Follow-through case study of clinical supervision, A report to the Educational Research and Development Committee, Canberra, November 1982

Smyth, J., Clinical Supervision - Collaborative Learning About Teaching, Geelong: Deakin University Press, 1984(a)

Smyth, J., Developing a critical practice of clinical supervision, Paper presented to the Annual Meeting of American Educational Research Association, New Orleans, April 1984(b)

Smyth, J., Toward a 'critical consciousness' in the instructional supervision of experienced teachers, Curriculum Inquiry, 14, (4), 1984(c), 425-436

Snyder, K., Clinical supervision in the 1980's, Educational Leadership, 38, (7), April 1981, 521-24

Sullivan, C., Clinical Supervision: A State of the Art Review, Alexandria, Va: Association for Supervision & Curriculum Development, 1980

Chapter 6

SITUATIONAL ANALYSIS OF TEACHING IN CLINICAL SUPERVISION

Brent Kilbourn

Introduction

The basic conception of clinical supervision and actual instances of its practice are problematic. The conception is problematic because of the usual difficulties of definition that attend practical work. What are the defining attributes of the craft? What kinds of evidence should count as indicators of successful clinical practice and how should improvement be monitored and judged? These kinds of questions are issues of definition but they are significant because the nature of the answers helps shape practice. The practice of clinical supervision is problematic because of the usual tension between ideal and real. Respect for the teacher's autonomy may be a defining attribute of the craft, but what counts as adequately and appropriately fulfilling this attribute may be open to question in a given clinical situation. It makes little sense to discuss either conceptual or empirical issues in the absence of cases of practice, or at least in the absence of certain kinds of data arising from practical situations. Articulating the boundaries of clinical supervision and the rules of thumb which guide its practice in a way helpful to others engaging the process, 'will depend largely on the wisdom gained from studying specific cases of clinical supervision since it is specific instances of clinical practice, complete with historical background, that give life and meaning to the process' (Kilbourn, 1982, p.2).

This chapter will contribute to the discussion by addressing three issues. The first concerns the appropriate attitude toward the observation of teaching in clinical supervision.

The second concerns the question of what should be the substantive foci of clinical supervision. The third concerns the nature of the data appropriate to clinical practice and research on clinical practice.

Several qualifiers are in order: I will not be dealing with the interactive process in clinical supervision. Critical though the teacher-supervisor relationship may be, this chapter is aimed at the question of: what classroom events are worthy of attention? Even so, it is important to recognise that I am looking at the interactive process as non-manipulative professional development, distinct from formal and informal performance evaluation. The shape I give to the issues emerges from experience with middle and senior school settings.

Situational Attitude

There are two very different attitudes from which to look at classroom teaching: categorical and situational. I shall argue that a situational attitude should be a defining characteristic of clinical supervision.

The categorical attitude occurs when established categories are brought to the observation and are held constant. Teaching events are looked at only through the lens of the categories with the categories themselves often being constructed in such a way as to enable the observer to quantify the results (eg. amount of praise; number of divergent questions; amount of time-on-task; number of correct responses; etc). The use of category systems for conceptualising classroom events in empirical research frequently exhibits a penchant for quantification. The epistemological requirements of the research require quantification (among other things) in order to rigorously substantiate the claims that are made. Because of their fixed and quantifiable nature, the categories support a stance toward observation that ignores the interrelated and dynamic nature of human events, and issues of quality and worth - for instance:

- What is the nature of this event?
- How appropriate is it, given the situation?
- How well is it done?

These are questions not addressed by a categorical attitude toward the observation of teaching. Whether for purposes of research or observational feedback, the use of static categories means that the categories themselves come to dominate the classroom situations to which they are applied. Examining teaching through pre-specified categories lends itself to maxims about teaching ('the teacher should always...') which are prone to be understood in terms of quantity rather than quality. Intended or not, standard supervisory checklists are frequently used in this way.

In contrast, a situational attitude toward teaching takes the events of any given situation as primary. The nature of the events that characterise a situation are central in the attempt to understand the situation on its own terms. The context within which events occur is important and includes the intentions of the participants and the unique circumstances of the particular moment. In the situational view of teaching qualitative issues are foremost. There is a tendency to ask questions like: Given the circumstances and the intentions of the teacher is this particular instance of interaction appropriate, handled well, productive, etc.,? Issues of quantity arise only insofar as they are critical for understanding a situation. A situational attitude to teaching has strong ties to an anthropological research tradition.

Kilbourn (1980) has outlined the close relationship between clinical supervision and ethnographic modes of research. Roberts (1982) has elaborated the difference between quantitative and qualitative research along the same lines as the above distinction; namely, between 'scientific' (experimental, empirical/statistical) and 'anthropological' (ethnographic, naturalistic) research, Roberts argues that different research modes have different metaphysical roots, and uses Stephen Pepper's (1942) work to show that the roots of quantitative research lie in Formism and Mechanism, while the roots of qualitative research lie in Contextualism and Organicism. He shows that differences in modes of research are rooted in peoples' attitude toward the nature of reality - their world view.

My outine of categorical and situational attitudes toward classroom observation can also be seen in terms of world view. The categorical attitude suggests the pre-eminence of categories as ideal forms, characteristic of Formism, and tends to emphasise quantitative issues, characteristic of Mechanism. The metaphor of 'situation' emphasises the context of particular events, characteristic of Contextualism; and even commonplace notions of 'situation' imply the integration-of-parts, typical of Organicism. As with different research modes, different attitudes toward observation can be seen as closely connected to views about reality.

Although in clinical practice it is important to let categories and issues 'emerge from the situation', it is also true that the constellation of explicit and implicit categories that we bring to the situation as clinical supervisors influences in a variety of ways what we are prepared to see and how we will see it. A situational attitude toward the observation of teaching does not deny the use of categories for thinking about the teaching act but, if taken seriously, it pushes us to let the situation exert considerable control on what categories are taken to be relevant and how those categories are to be shaped. A situational attitude demands that we be flexible by insisting that our categories and thinking be responsive to change as the situation progresses. Donald Schon's (1983) work is helpful for understanding aspects of a situational attitude toward events. According to Schon, in practical settings a practitioner (e.g., a teacher or a participant/observer of teaching) is always dealing with a particular situation which is 'framed':

> When we set the problem, we select what we will treat as the 'things' of the situation, we set the boundaries of our attention to it, and we impose upon it a coherence which allows us to say what is wrong and in what directions the situation needs to be changed. Problem setting is a process in which interactively, we name the things to which we will attend and frame the context in which we will attend to them (p.40).

The act of framing a situation depends on the repertoire which the practitioner brings to the situation. This repetoire consists of 'categories' in the broadest sense - remembered instances, images, metaphors, vignettes, interpreted events, etc. - in short, all manner of experience. According to Schon (1983):

> When a practitioner makes sense of a situation he perceives to be unique, he sees it as something already present in his repertoire (p. 138) ... The artistry of a practitioner ... hinges on the range and variety of the repertoire that he brings to unfamiliar situations. Because he is able to see these as elements of his repertoire, he is able to make sense of their uniquenss and need not reduce them to instances of standard categories. (p. 140)

Obviously, one limiting factor to such reflective practice is the adequacy of the categories which are brought to the situation and are used to frame it. If those categories are wanting, the extent to which a situation can be fruitfully dealt with is likely to be limited. Schon (1983) sketches several ways of addressing the limits to reflective practice:

> A practitioner might break into a circle of self-limiting reflection by attending to his role frame, his interpersonal theory-in-use, or the organizational learning system in which he functions. Whatever his starting point, however, he is unlikely to get very far unless he wants to extend and deepen his reflection-in-action, and <u>unless others help him to see what he has worked to avoid seeing</u> (my emphasis, p. 282-283).

The 'will-to-act' is a necessary component for reflective practice, but Schon's (1983) other point (emphasised above) is also important. Clinical supervision can be seen as a process in which the primary role of the participant/observer (supervisor) is to help the teacher reflect on teaching practice. If the role of the supervisor is seen in terms of reflective practice then one function of the role is to work with the teacher on developing ways of framing a situation which grow out of the situation, are responsive to it, and which have reasonable scope for enhancing it. (Not all situations need enhancing, of course, but this fact does not alter the supervisor's role - what has worked well and why in a particular situation is as much a topic for reflection as what has not worked well.) How well a supervisor is able to conduct this aspect of the role depends in part on the supervisor's repertoire, and that repertoire must be rich in terms of teaching, the observation of teaching, and working with teachers. The clinical supervisor must be engaged in reflective practice with regard to the act of supervision. In fact, in both teaching and clinical supervision, the judgement of appropriateness of action can profitably be seen in terms of an epistemology of practice where careful attention is paid to the particulars of specific situations.

Understanding and articulating an appropriate attitude to be taken towards the observation of teaching in clinical supervision is important because it helps us deal with slips between espoused views of practice and practice itself. There are at least three defining attributes to the spirit of clinical supervision:

- respect for the teacher's autonomy;
- respect for evidence in terms of the particulars of a given teaching act; and,
- respect for the historical and contextual continuity of the entire process (Kilbourn, 1982).

Satisfactory fulfilment of these is a necessary (but not sufficient) condition if one is to be seriously engaged in clinical supervision. It should be apparent that a situational attitude toward the observation of teaching underlies these vital attributes of clinical supervision and is inherrent in the concept of 'clinical'.

There are two different kinds of limitation which relate to the supervisor's repertoire for attending to clinical supervisory situations. One concerns the attitude taken toward observation. The more the supervisor drifts from a situational view toward a categorical one, the more the process drifts from fulfilling essential features of clinical practice. This is not to suggest that the supervisor does not have categories which serve as building blocks for interpreting and framing new situations. For every supervisor these categories form a repertoire (in Schon's sense) which provides issues for the supervisor to be prepared to look at in teaching, which can be used to frame a teaching situation, and which can be used to develop unique interpretations as the teaching situation demands. A second limitation to the supervisor's performance, then, concerns the adequacy of the categories brought to the teaching situation and used for framing it. If the supervisor's general understanding of the teaching act is simplistic or skewed, then the ability to respond adequately to a demanding situation may be limited.

A View of Teaching

Are there any particular categories that a supervisor should bring to the interpretation of teaching situations? Put more broadly, is there a point of view about teaching which has priority in guiding the construction and use of other interpretive categories? In this portion of the chapter I shall argue for a point of view about teaching which emanates from conceptual analyses of 'teaching' and which, in my judgment, should underlie the framing and interpretation of many teaching situations. Komisar's (1968) analysis will be used to carry the features of the view, although it should be clear that the view is not restricted to his terminology. Neither is Komisar's position restrictive in terms of teaching methodology. He makes no claims about how certain kinds of teaching acts <u>should</u> be done. This is essential for respecting the teacher's autonomy and for maintaining a situational attitude toward observation. Komisar's analysis reminds us that certain things in the empirical observation of teaching stem from the meaning of the concept itself.

According to Komisar (1968) the term 'teaching' can refer simply to an occupation ('She is teaching this year, but next year is going to graduate school'). The enterprise sense of 'teaching' is used more precisely to refer to many things we do as teachers while on the job, like order books, supervise the lunch-room, take roll, etc. The distinction between teaching-as-occupation and teaching-as-enterprise allows us to say without contradiction, 'I am teaching (this year), but I am not teaching today (it is a holiday).' An even more precise sense of the term refers more particularly to the things we typically do when we are actively teaching something to someone. This act of 'teaching' is what Komisar (1968) sees as the point of the whole occupation and enterprise. The distinction between teaching-as-enterprise and teaching-as-act allows us to say 'I am teaching (this morning) but I am not teaching now (I am monitoring the hall).'

Komisar (1968) suggests three possible kinds of teaching acts (learning-donor, learner-enhancing, and intellectual). Learning-donor acts are those 'intended to contribute rather directly and pointedly to the production of learning. Acts that appear to be of this kind are prompting, cueing, reinforcing, drilling, censuring or censoring, approving, showing, etc.'(p. 75). Learner-enhancing acts are those 'intended to put or maintain the learner in a fit state to receive instruction. Included among acts done to make the student 'learningable' are those intended to reduce anxiety, alleviate perceptual deficiencies, arouse interest, focus attention, and those often talked of as ego strengthening'(p. 75). Many management and control issues can be seen as species of learner-enhancing acts. It should be clear that in many, if not most, teaching situations learning-donor acts and learning-enhancing acts are not ends in themselves but are in the service of the intellectual acts of teaching. Intellectual acts include demonstrating, questioning, explicating, hypothesising, appraising, and rating, to name a few of Komisar's examples (p. 76). These acts are central to the students' awareness and learning and, therefore, are often the whole point of teaching. 'The strictest, the basic, the keenest concept of teaching we have is the concept we apply to designate particular occurrences of intellectual acts directed to the auditor' (Komisar, 1968, p. 88)

With regard to clinical supervision the conversations between the teacher and the supervisor may concern any of the senses of 'teaching,' as the situation demands. At times the conversation may involve talk at the occupation or enterprise level, but because clinical supervision is conventionally conceived as focussing on classroom interaction, the conversation is often focussed on the various teaching acts. Komisar's analysis, relating to the observation of teaching, is important because it reminds us of the centrality of intellectual acts. In many teaching situations the ultimate goal is to affect the intellectual awareness of the learner. The supervisor is remiss if this fact is not taken into account in reflecting on the teaching situation. (There are some possible exceptions to the centrality of intellectual acts, although I shall not go into them in detail. One concerns the teaching of physical and aesthetic skills; another concerns the emphasis on learner-enhancing acts in early primary school; and another concerns situations where the point of teaching is to have the students go through some form of personal experience).

Although intellectual acts may be central to teaching, and, therefore, a keen understanding of them should be part of the supervisor's repertoire, there remains the question of what it is that a supervisor should be attending to when considering the intellectual character of an instance of teaching. What distinguishes intellectual acts like 'rating', 'appraising', or 'hypothesising' from learner-enhancing and learner-donor acts which also bear an intimate relationship to the teacher's effort to help students learn? More simply, what are 'the defining characteristics, the criteria for intellectual acts of teaching?' (Komisar, 1968, p. 76). Komisar (1968) argues that intellectual acts of teaching are characterised by their <u>logical lucidity</u>:

> Generally, though not too clearly, intellectual acts are logically lucid in that the act is done not only with the intention of securing a certain 'uptake' (an awareness of some point), but also so as (a) to divulge to the student what the intention is and (b) to achieve his awareness by identifying the reasons given as the intelligible grounds for the point the students are to become aware of. Finally, neither a nor b is essential to the overall enterprise of teaching (or other teaching acts) (pp. 79-80).

According to Komisar, the criterion of logical lucidity is important because this is how intellectual teaching acts can be distinguished from 'cousins to teaching,' such as indoctrinating, deceiving, or training (p. 81).

Komisar himself seems to admits that the criterion of logical lucidity is not easy to grasp, but in commonplace ways we can begin to understand what it might mean. For example, we might ask of some teaching episodes: Is this clear? Are the critical parts of the argument in place? Is this train of thought intelligible? Does this make sense?, and so on. These kinds of questions speak to the issue of logical lucidity and they are important because they address the question of the extent to which an intellectual teaching act can reasonably be judged as being meaningful and understandable by the student. Komisar identifies 'providing reasons' as one aspect of logical lucidity; we can imagine episodes of teaching in which giving reasons why such and such is the case, or why so and so is a reasonable way to proceed, are manifest in the interaction. Green (1968) adopts a position compatible with Komisar's notion of logical lucidity. He argues that non-indoctrinatory teaching involves a 'conversation of instruction':

> Instruction seems, at heart, to involve a kind of conversation, the object of which is to give reasons, weigh evidence, justify, explain, conclude, and so forth (p. 32).
>
> The point is not, therefore, that instructing necessarily requires communication. The point is rather that it requires a certain kind of communication and that kind is the kind which includes giving reasons, evidence, argument, etc., in order to approach the truth. The importance of this fact can be seen if we consider what happens when the conversation of instruction is centred less and less upon this kind of communication. It takes no great powers of insight to see that in proportion as the conversation of instruction is less and less characterised by argument, reasons, objections, explanations, and so forth, in proportion as it is less and less directed towards an apprehension of truth, it more and more closely resembles what we call indoctrination (p. 33).

The criterion of logical lucidity for intellectual acts of teaching does not presuppose any particular method or model of teaching (although logical lucidity may be more easily achieved with some models than others). We can readily imagine it as being evident in whole class discussion, small group work, lecture, and so on. Nor does the criterion say anything about who should be doing what at any given time in a teaching situation. In some instances we might find the teacher giving reasons, explaining, justifying, while in other instances these features would characterise student discourse. We could be talking about teacher directed work or an activity which the students have formulated and engaged. In either case it is appropriate to ask about the intellectual point of the interaction and the extent to which it meets a criterion of logical lucidity. Finally, the criterion of logical lucidity says nothing about the degree to which it should be manifested in a given situation. Common sense suggests that it would be inappropriate to demand that reasons be given in every instance where reasons could be given. This latter point foreshadows the issues to be taken up in the next section of the chapter.

Exemplification

I have argued that, although the spirit of clinical supervision entails a situational attitude toward the observation of teaching, it is only natural for the supervisor to bring a repertoire of categories (images and experiences) to the teaching situation. I have also argued that a point-of-view about teaching which respects its intellectual character should be included in the supervisor's repertoire because this point-of-view is inherent in fundamental aspects of what it means to teach in a democratic society, and because many empirical instances of teaching by their very nature are intellectual teaching acts. This is a modest position - it only says that a point of view about teaching which recognises the place of logically lucid intellectual acts of teaching should be in the supervisor's professional repertoire and that there are aspects of many teaching situations which demand to be interpreted (partially, at least) in this light. While this position is suggestive of aspects of the supervisor's interpretation of relevant teaching situations, it says nothing about the teacher's role in interpretation, nothing about prescriptions to the situation (developed by the supervisor, the teacher, or both), and it says nothing about the nature of the interaction between the teacher and the supervisor.

My sense of the importance of intellectual acts of teaching and an effort to make them logically lucid goes beyond an abstract philosophical principle. Logical lucidity is important insofar as it relates to students' ability to develop meaning and make sense of their classsroom experiences. It should be clear that a point-of-view about teaching which incorporates a notion about the logical lucidity of intellectual acts is something I think should be in the professional repertoires of both teachers and supervisors. What is not clear is how, as clinical supervisors, we should inform ourselves about this particular point-of-view (or some other point-of-view, dealing with either the substance or process of teaching and clinical supervision). It is not clear because of what might be called the problem of 'exemplification'. The practice of clinical supervision can thrive only when the discussion of abstractions is grounded in data from particular situations. Certain questions become inescapable: What counts as an instance of logical lucidity? What does an issue of logical lucidity look like when we see it? What is the 'feel' of the issue as it relates to sayings and doings of a teacher and students in a particular situation? It is only by discussing the particulars of given cases that we can begin to develop an understanding of what an issue of logical lucidity might look like so that we can add this category to our professional repertoire, in order to recognise the issue in fresh teaching situations when appropriate.

The following discussion of a teaching situation will demonstrate the concept of logical lucidity and show how the concept is central to the interpretation of the situation. Although the discussion will be focussed on logical lucidity, more generally it will indicate one kind of issue to be addressed in research on clinical supervision (What counts as an instance of...?), and of the kind of data relevant to such research. The following account does not attend to all of the data which is pertinent to the teaching situation. I have selected aspects to highlight the issue of logical lucidity - the larger context of the situation is a point I shall revisit toward the end of the chapter.

The analysed excerpts below are from the transcript of a secondary school literature lesson. Students had been asked to do a piece of creative writing. On the day of the lesson they were asked to read their work and let their classmates judge its quality. The operational structure of the lesson involved reading a work, followed by teacher-directed class discussion of the work, followed by a class vote. This cycle occurred five times in the lesson. The intellectual structure of the lesson can be seen in terms of aesthetic appraisal. Proceeding along the lines of Toulmin's (1969) 'argument pattern' such appraisal involves at least three basic components. There are the data, represented by the oral readings of students' writing, there are the conclusions about the data which constitute the appraisal itself (which, in this case, are symbolised by a class vote), finally, there are the warrants or criteria which are used to logically move from the data to the conclusions. When used appropriately the criteria help insure the adequacy of the appraisal. It is well within the spirit of Komisar's account to say that there must be criteria, they must be relatively clear, and they must be used appropriately if we are to say that the intellectual act of appraising is logically lucid. Simply put, students have to be able to see the grounds on which an appraisal has been made. At the beginning of the lesson the teacher outlines the basis for appraising student entries:

1. T: I've put something on the board to help you in the judging of entries and we might discuss it very briefly. How much value should we put on to each one of these suggested ideas? You have the title, the opening sentence, the opening idea, content of the total story, the interest of it and so on, the originality, the fluency of the language - now that includes appropriateness of words, fluency of sentences, so you don't have too much repetition - things that we've done before of that nature. And the ending,

how good is the ending? Now if you look at those five suggestions, which strikes you as the most important? Jack?

2. Jack: Um, the content, almost half.

3. T: I think the content, yes. Alright, so we have five suggested ideas for judging the entries. Jack is suggesting that the content should be worth close to half, approximately half. Agreed? That should help you in judging ...

With regard to the interchange (1-3) above there is a question as to the extent to which the students have actually been given adequate criteria for making the intellectual act of appraising logically lucid for them. The 'title', for example, is more a 'category-to-be-looked-at' than it is a criterion, and a student might reasonably ask 'what should I pay attention to when I think about the title?' The answer to that question would likely begin to address criteria. Alternatively, all of the concepts might be seen as criteria, some of which are more specific than others. The question then turns on the extent to which they are specific enough to enable a sound appraisal. For example, 'interest' and 'originality' might be seen as criteria underlying the more general category of 'content'. But on what grounds are students to judge something to be 'original'? After several teacher/student interchanges, Jack reads his story:

4. Jack: 'The Most Expensive Bowl of Soup.'

A year ago I had a strange experience. At the Mission they were giving out free meals to all that came. There were four in line, all hungry. The first one went in and came out with a styrofoam bowl full of soup. Just as the last one came out, a man jumped out of a Rolls Royce and walked up to the kitchen. As he came out I asked him 'You are pretty well dressed for someone going to take free lunches.' He replied. 'Why not, my cook makes awful lunches and I put all my money in a savings account. Then I forgot the number to take it out! So that now I can't take any money out until Irene, the new clerk, comes back and tells her boss that I really do have an account.' I felt surprised. The next year I heard that a certain Howard Hughes had donated five hundred dollars to the Mission.

5. T: Well, how does that strike you? As the total now, as the total story, how does that strike you?
6. Karen: Not clear enough
7. T: Ah, what is unclear, what strikes you as unclear? What would you like clarified?
8. Karen: Ah, he says the title, but you really have to remember the title right through the story to get the ending.
9. T: The title tells what the whole story is about. What is the title again?
10. Jack: 'The Most Expensive Bowl of Soup'
11. T: How does that tie together with the ending ?
12. Karen: Well, its just that he donated five hundred dollars for a bowl of soup.
13. T: Alright, it was voluntary, right? Does the title contribute to the story?
14. Debby: Yes.
15. T: Yes, it's a necessary part.
16. Rita: But you have to remember it again to, uh - I read it before but had to look at the title again to get it.
17. T: And when you did, you understood it. Alright, I don't know that we should criticise that because if a title is a vital part of the story it does contribute, then it seems to be alright.

Karen brings up the issue of the title (interchange 8). The teacher alludes to an implicit criterion in 9 and 11. By 13 and 17 the teacher's criterion more transparently concerns the contribution of the title to the story. However, Karen (8) and Rita (16) seem to be using implicit criteria concerning how memorable and clear the title is. The teacher continues:

18. T: How is the plot? How do you feel about the plot? Do you feel it's original?
19. Brian: Yeah !
20. T: Yes, alright, how about fluency of language ?

21. Beth: At the beginning the first man came out - he came out and he came out again.
22. T: I suppose some fluency could be worked on, but the story comes through alright. Did the opening sentence strike you with something that you'd want to continue? Could you read the opening again ?
23. Jack: A year ago I had a strange experience.
24. T: What do you think? Do you want to hear the strange experience? What about the ending sentence, could you read that?
25. Jack: The next year I heard that a certain Howard Hughes had donated five hundred dollars to the Mission.
26. T: Well, what do you think?
27. Ted: It explains everything.
28. T: It explains everything and it is like a big impressive period. So the construction of the story seems alright, doesn't it?

In interchanges 18-28 the teacher introduces the categories and mentions a criterion for the judgment of each: For plot, the criterion is originality (18); for fluency, the criterion is intelligibility ('the story comes through alright') (22); for opening sentence, the criterion is interest ('something that you'd want to continue') (22-24); for ending sentence, the criterion is satisfying explanation (28). In all of these instances the criteria are used by the teacher but not explicitly talked about as criteria. Nor are the applications of the criteria of equal difficulty. For example, for a student the criterion 'interest' is likely to be more easily determined than 'originality' since the former is usually determined in-relation-to-oneself whereas the latter implicitly refers to a standard or to other writings. The teacher turns to the task of judging Jack's story:

29. T: Well, do you want to judge now? What do you think? The red or blue? The red is for something superior, the blue for something good, acceptable. How many vote for blue? How many vote for red? The rest of you are chickens who don't want to make up your mind. It looks like Jack has a red and he has a good original story. I do agree that

perhaps some of the sentences need a bit of smoothing out, and also it really has a great deal to do with how you read it. Doesn't it? ...

Several issues are worthy of note here. Theoretically, the quality of writing might represent a continuum from excellent to poor (with any number of specified gradations), but the choice allows only two points on the continuum. The two choices are not bipolar but could easily be interpreted as such by the students. The vote for red or blue is made difficult by the fact that there is no explicit or implicit standard or point of reference. Implicit standards frequently develop with the kind of experience likely unacquired by these students. Finally, this is the first hint that some students are reluctant to evaluate their peers. After several interchanges another student reads:

30. Debby: 'Rebellion'
I had to write about me.
But me didn't want to.
Rebellious I have to be
I had to be brave,
To face the anger.
That might arise,
From defying the teacher,
Who wanted to pry.
To pry into me,
Who'd been pried before,
And who wanted no more.

There is some discussion about the meaning of the poem, followed by:

31. T: Alright, does her idea come through clearly?

32. Julie: Yes, at the end of the last sentence, the rhythm, like it all goes - the rhythm is very good till the last sentence. That ending sentence doesn't fit in with the rest of the rhythm.

33. T: That's true, except I would put it differently. I thought that the rhythm and the rhyme was better at the end than it was in the middle. That hadn't been quite worked out as smoothly as it might be, but I thought at the end it rhymes doesn't it? It sort of makes it

stronger. Does the rhyme at the end add something? I think so. Alright, title: good, appropriate?
34. Karen: Yes.
35. T: Yes. The opening? Effective, interesting?

Several interchanges occur concerning the meaning of the poem.

36. T: Alright. The content we all agreed was very good, very original. Fluency?
37. Jack: I thought that around the middle, there was something ...
38. T: Does it sound smooth all the way through?
39. Bob: No.
40. T: As long as she rhymed it in the end, should there not be some kind of regular pattern? That seems to be missing. What do you think is more important in that poem, the thought or the form?
41. Steve: The thought.
42. T: The thought and that comes out better, doesn't it? The ending? We all agreed that was different. Are we ready to judge? Red? Opposed? It is unanimous?
43. Students: Yes.

On the whole, the teacher is doing most of the intellectual work. That is, it is the teacher who offers and uses the criteria. For example, in 42 the teacher says that 'we all agreed that [the ending] was different' and yet such agreement seems to stem from the teacher's own utterances in 33 and 40. Julie is the only student who contributes an opinion in her own words (32) and that does not support the teacher's view (42). After 43, the teacher says to Debby:

44. T: How do you feel about smoothing it out and polishing it for fluency?
45. Debby: Well ...
46. Ted: It may lose its effect.
47. T: You don't think it would be hers as much.
48. Ted: I think that it is good just like that.
49. T: You like it just like that ?
50. Bob: The whole poem is about rebellion. It's her own way of writing it, so if

anyone wants to change it's rebellion.

51\. T: Good for you! Someone is prying, someone is trying to reshape. Here is another topic for you: someone who is constantly wanting to reshape what you do. Alright, very good. So we agreed to a red for Debby.

The student resistance and subsequent outcome seen in 44-51 is only partly related to the lack of clear criteria for judging the issue of fluency. A more comprehensive situational analysis would have to take into account the meaning of the poem itself as it relates to the total dynamics of the situation. The next piece is read:

52\. Julie: 'Snowballs'
Throwing snowballs is lots of fun
When all the girls scream and run
With dripping faces, pants and coats
Freezing snow even down your throat.

Getting hit in the head
With an iceball that feels like lead
Trying to get this person back
Instead of getting mad and blowing your stack.
Pulling your arm back
To make it fly
And watch it hit
The teacher's eye.

Getting in trouble
Playing some more
Practising shooting
At the first door.

Once again the season ends
And you and your friends
Must make amends.

After some discussion about the theme:

53\. T: Title?
54\. Ken: It's original.
55\. T: 'Snowballs.' Well, it is a very common title like 'Old Shoe' but it's the treatment of it. Ordinary, common or original?
56\. Ken: Original.

57. T: It's very original.

Ken says the title is original (54) which is contradicted by the teacher's assertion that it is common (55). This interchange is significant in terms of logical lucidity because there are no criteria for what counts as 'originality: and no reasons are given by Ken or the teacher for their conclusions. The lack of reasons provides little opportunity for adjudication when the teacher and a student disagree on a matter of interpretation. 'Originality' is treated in polar terms even though it is a matter of degree; and the lack of a standard of comparison tends to steer a listener to the previous work. A moment's reflection suggests that the works 'Snowballs' (52) and 'Rebellion' (30) are original in different senses or to different degrees.

I shall close this brief analysis with a comment on the nature and extent of student participation. There are several pieces of data in the transcript which are relevant. The first occurs in 29 when the teacher says 'The rest of you are chickens who don't want to make up your mind.' The second occurs at the end of the discussion on 'Snowballs' (52):

58. T: Ready to judge?
59. Frank: Red
60. T: My but you're generous today. Alright.

The third occurs toward the end of discussion of the next story called 'Switchblade Mania'.

61. T: I think we agree that one could use a bit of polishing and clarification of detail. Shall we judge? Suggestions? What do we do? Jack?
62. Jack: I don't really know.
63. Ted: Well, it has to be either red for superior, blue for good, acceptable, or it has to be reworked in which case we would hold our judgement. So what do we do ?
64. Ted: Well, we could judge now but if he works it over he could get a red tomorrow.
65. Julie: I agree with that.
66. T: Do you all agree or do we vote? How many people agree? Some of you aren't even paying attention. Do you agree

that we give him a blue but that he may rework it if he wishes?

67. Ss: Yeah, yes ...

These interchanges suggest that the teacher feels some student's appraisals are less than discriminating (60), and that students are somewhat reluctant to evalute their peers' work (29, 62-66). One hypothesis for these interpretations is that the students are engaged in an intellectual act which is not logically lucid to them. The 'ground rules' for linking the data to conclusions about the data are not all that clear, and under those conditions the students are publicly placed in a 'high risk' situation.

In this portion of the chapter I have exemplified the issue of logical lucidity for two reasons. First, logical lucidity is a defining characteristic of intellectual acts which, in turn, are central to the concept of teaching and to many teaching situations. In these situations logical lucidity sets a standard to which teaching should aspire. Second, central though logical lucidity may be to teaching, what counts as an issue of logical lucidity in actual practice is much less clear. Discussion of an attribute of teaching like logical lucidity will serve the practice of clinical supervision well only if it moves at some point to reflection on actual teaching situations. These situations allow us to see varying degrees of the manifestation of an attribute and provide a context for imagining how the attribute could be enhanced. The instance of teaching above can and should be interpreted in terms of the logical lucidity of the intellectual acts of teaching in the situation. (I trust it is understood that I am not referring to the specific terminology I have used in the analysis; nor am I referring even to the specific shape of the analysis). I am not suggesting that the point-of-view taken in the analysis is the only way that the situation can or should be interpreted. I am claiming, however, that a clinical supervisor fails to understand this teaching episode unless he or she sees the structure of the act of appraising, the related parts to that structure, and the roles of the teacher and students as they engage that structure.

In short, the point of view represented in the analysis is necessary, but not sufficient, for understanding the lesson. It says nothing about how the teacher and supervisor might work together, including what issues might be broached. And it says very little about specific ways in which the lesson might be enhanced, if it should be enhanced. For example, the outcome of the analysis does not mean that providing detailed criteria is the only (or even the most reasonable) tack to take in the lesson. The lack of clear criteria made it difficult for the teacher and Ken to adjudicate their disagreement over the originality of the title 'Snowballs' (53-55) in terms other than power. But that does not mean that generalised criteria for 'originality' would be helpful since their development and use would be pedagogically difficult and possibly inappropriate (because highly detailed aesthetic criteria are frequently context specific). The spirit of logical lucidity would have been served had the teacher responded to Ken's claim (54) by saying something like: 'In what sense do you mean 'original'?' We might then have found that Ken was actually talking about the content of the poem rather than the title. Or we might have found that Ken did have reasons for thinking the title was original. And we might envision the teacher helping Ken to develop and articulate those reasons. In these hypothesised instances the teacher's questions and probes would be aimed at making the interaction more logically lucid by elucidating the reasons which link the conclusion to the data.

Situation and Supervision

Central though intellectual acts may be to many teaching situations, they are not the sole concern of the teacher or clinical supervisor. The following will point to several contextual features that would likely be relevant if the supervisor were to attend more fully to the idea of 'situation.' The brevity of the discussion bears no relationship to the relative importance of these features as they relate to teaching and learning situations. Some of the features would concern historical context lying outside the classroom such as the kind of school and the biographies of the teacher and students. Some would concern historical context within the class such as the nature of previous work. And, with regard to the sample lesson in this chapter, there are many additional features of the lesson itself which likely would be salient to a more comprehensive understanding of the situation. For example, non-verbal features as well as how many students were in the class, how many participated, who participated, how often, and what was the nature of the participation are all relevant to the situation. As outlined above, there is evidence that students were reluctant to participate and this interpretation was partially explained by the lack of clear criteria for making aesthetic appraisals.

However, Komisar's (1968) idea of learner-enhancing acts is also useful for directing attention to features of the situation relevant to clinical supervision. If part of the teaching act is to put the learner in a fit state to receive instruction by, for example, reducing anxiety, then the relationship between the nature of the learning task and the culture of high-school students is important context. Public evaluation of one's peers or their work, in their presence, is well beyond the comfort range of most high-school students. The formal voting ('red/blue') in this lesson works against an affectively supportive learning environment and, interestingly, is not necessary to the intellectual act of aesthetic appraisal which is the thrust of the lesson.

'Voting' may be seen as an issue of strategy critical to the effective environment of the class. Serious questions are also raised if we turn to the appropriateness of the intellectual acts themselves. Those of us who might react unfavourably to 'voting' might similarly question the wisdom of the teacher appraising students' creative efforts, or of students appraising each others work, of the manner of appraisal, or of making appraisals public. I shall not address the ideological issues that might underly such concerns but wish to call attention to another relevant aspect of context. A central feature of this lesson and of its critique in clinical supervision involves the intentions of the teacher. A list is not difficult to imagine - the intent of this lesson could have been for students to:

- practise the skills of creative writing;
- use constructive criticism to improve writing;
- learn the skills of aesthetic criticism;

- develop criteria for aesthetic criticism;
- learn to accept criticism;
- learn to listen critically ...

While these goals are not mutually exclusive, each one alters the complexion of the situation by providing a different context for addressing the appropriateness of the intellectual tasks and for addressing fitting images of logical lucidity. The fact that the goals have not been explicitly discussed in the lesson suggests a twist on Komisar's notion of logical lucidity. The possibility that the students lack a clear understanding of the substantive reasons why they are doing what they are doing indicates that pedagogical lucidity may also be relevant to an understanding of this situation.

To this point the focus has been on those aspects of the situation relative to what the teacher could or should be doing with students. The discussion has been as though the supervisor were a detached observer, separated from the teaching situation. However, the craft of clinical supervision needs to be guided by a broader conception of situation - one in which prominent features include the teacher's views of the lesson, the teacher's history of supervision, the nature of the relationship between the teacher and the supervisor, and the nature of the changing understandings about substance and process (by teacher and supervisor) as supervision moves through time. The supervisor's view of how his/her role should appropriately be enacted must respect the situation qua teaching and qua supervision. For example, at a given point in the supervisory process a supervisor might find framing aspects of this lesson in terms of the logical lucidity of intellectual acts not particularly useful for helping the teacher make sense of the situation. The supervisor may decide not to broach the issue of intellectual act or may decide to approach it in a particular way, depending on how the teacher is oriented to the teaching situation and the supervisory situation.

Conclusion

If clinical supervision is conceived as a process guided by an epistemology of reflective practice, then one of the central functions of research on the process is to provide a rich set of categories for reflecting on instances of practice and for contributing to the supervisor's knowledge and skills. One kind of relevant research would be characterised by case studies of various aspects of clinical practice. Case studies would have the potential for contributing to images of how to practise the craft as well as images of what the craft should be. In dealing with the question of the substantive foci of clinical supervision this chapter has addressed the intellectual act of teaching as only one of a number of aspects of teaching and supervision that are worthy of attention. Of course there is much more that could be said about the intellectual dimension than the brief account in this chapter, and subsequent cases might emphasise different intellectual issues. Some cases might highlight learner-enhancing acts by attending to the emotional climate of the classroom, or issues of management and control. Other cases might take the nature of the interaction between teacher and supervisor as their primary concern and here, the meaning (in practice) of respect for the teacher's autonomy might be a dominant feature of the discussion. Still others might elaborate the way in which all of these dimensions are fused in practice and how understanding the nature of that fusion is essential in clinical practice.

A final comment, implicit in the lesson analysis above, concerns the nature of the case study data in research on clinical supervision. As in practice, that data needs to be highly specific in terms of who said and did what, and when, where, and how. An ethnographic research paradigm with its implict world view of context and integration is fitting for research on clinical supervision. Not only is clarity needed concerning the categories used for interpreting teaching and supervisory situations, those categories need to be exemplified in recounted instances of practice. Recounted instances enable the supervisor to reflect on clinical supervisory practice and assist the construction of images of improved practice. The nature of the detail, in a given instance of course, depends on the point which the case addresses. The detail in the lesson analysis above is sufficiently rich to exemplify the concept of logical lucidity but it is not adequate for exemplifying points about emotional climate. Relevant detail is necessary if case study research is to have meaning and appeal to practitioners and if reflection on clinical supervision is to move beyond espoused theory.

NOTE

Conversations with Douglas Barnes, Arthur Geddis, Thomas McCaul and John McCullock have contributed to the development of this chapter.

REFERENCES

Green, T., A topology of the teaching concept, In MacMillan & T. Nelson (eds.), Concepts of Teaching : Philosophical Essays, Chicago: Rand-McNally, 1968, 28-62

Kilbourn, B., Linda: a case-study in clinical supervision, Canadian Journal of Education, 7 (3), 1982, 1-24

Kilbourn, B., Ethnographic research and the improvement of teaching, In A.H. Munby, G. Orpwood, & T. Russell (eds.), Seeing Curriculum in A New Light: Essays from Science Education, Toronto : OISE Press, 1980

Komisar, P., Teaching: act and enterprise, In MacMillan & T. Nelson (eds), Concepts of Teaching: Philosophical Essays, Chicago: Rand-McNally, 1968, 63-88

Pepper, S., World Hypotheses, University of California Press, 1942

Roberts, D., The place of qualitative research in science education, Journal of Research in Science Teaching, 19 (4), 1982, 277-292

Schon, D., The Reflective Practitioner: How Professionals Think in Action, New York: Basic Books, 1983

Toulmin, S., The Uses of Argument, Cambridge University Press, 1958

Chapter 7

IS CLINICAL SUPERVISION PRACTICAL?

Lee Goldsberry

Other contributors to this book have spoken about the goals of clinical supervision, about the procedures necessary to make it work, and about the process itself and its results. But, does it always work? How might clinical supervision be started in a school to better its chances for success? This latter question forms the basis of this chapter with a series of sub-questions : What prerequisities are needed to initiate clinical supervision successfully? What preparation must be provided participants to maximise the likelihood of productive practice? What introduction of actual supervisory cycles seems likely to promote acceptance? And, how can clinical supervision programs be evaluated so as to encourage further growth. If this outline is construed as a tree with a number of branches, the filling out of limbs and foliage is largely left to the reader. Although a pine takes shape differently in Pennsylvania than in California or Texas or New South Wales, some principles of gardening are constant, and a competent and caring gardener who knows the local soil is invaluable for a successful transplant.

Prerequisites for Clinical Supervision

Just as suitable soil, temperate climate, and access to light are necessary for a pine, an appropriate mission, willing participation, and adequate resources are needed for clinical supervision. Of these, the first requirement is a clarity of mission. If the aim is to identify and harass substandard teachers, clinical supervision is not the right process. If the mission is to create a facade of 'everything is fine at our school,' then clinical supervision is the wrong tool. If the goal is to make some teachers look good, and others not so good - whether for pittances jocularly called 'merit pay' or not - then clinical supervision is inappropriate. Of course, any form of supervision intended for teachers has as its central (voiced) mission the improvement of teaching, and clinical supervision is no exception.

However, clinical supervision aims to do more. As Cogan (1973) put it :

> A central objective of the entire clinical process is the development of the professionally responsible teacher who is analytical of his own performance, open to help from others, and withal self-directing (p. 12).

Goldhammer (1969) used different words for the same notion :

> The supervision we envision is intended to increase teachers' incentives and skills for self-supervision and for supervising professional colleagues (p. 55).

In short, one feature which distinguishes clinical supervision from other approaches to working with teachers is its clear aim to develop within teachers the skills and dispositions necessary to evaluate one's own performance and to refine it whenever possible. This mission component endorses the preference that teachers possess the knowledge of learners and learning, as well as the organisationally sanctioned discretion to make decisions regarding teaching practice. If a school does not truly want teachers to consider the numerous and unpredictable variables that influence learning in a classroom situation and adapt their teaching accordingly - if a school prefers its teachers to rely on prescriptions for appropriate teaching behaviour general enough to be used in any teaching situation - then clinical supervision is contra-indicated.

The unfortunate truth is that too many reasonable approaches become so distorted in their delivery as to actually negate their original purposes. One need not revisit 'open education' or the curricular innovations of the early 1970's for support of this assertion. One need only witness a well-meaning administrator clinging to a too-short list of 'effective teaching' behaviours as she/he passes judgement on a lesson based on some frequency count of research-based teaching practices. This variation of supervision rarely examines the impact of the teaching tactics upon the learners in the classroom, the interactions of various teacher and student moves, the emotional tone of the setting, or the appropriateness of the teacher's goals. Rather than using research findings as springboards for examining the consequences of varied strategies designed to attain some specific benefit for learners, over-harried, and often ill-prepared educational administrators impose someone's correlates with achievement test scores as check-list standards for all to follow. In such settings independent and inquisitive behaviour is not sought from teachers - it is to be avoided.

When such 'leaders' of schools see teachers as technicians carrying out prescribed treatments without questioning the fit of the treatment to the setting or to the learners, clinical supervision is also to be avoided. When the official 'leaders' of schools see teachers as leaders themselves, adapting old treatments and discovering new ones as the need arises, clinical supervision can provide valuable help in that process. Nearly all 'leaders' espouse the latter position, even though we may question the sincerity of their actions.

While the clear aim of helping teachers exercise their prerogatives as educational decision-makers is the first prerequisite for a clinical supervision program, willing participation by supervisors and teachers is also necessary. Other contributors to this book, have portrayed clinical supervision as a form of collaborative problem-posing and problem-solving. Collaboration is easy to advocate ... for others. The difficult part of collaboration comes in giving discretion to one's collaborator, while maintaining personal committment to, and investment in, the products of the effort.

Collaboration for the clinical supervisor means taking pride in good teaching while crediting the teacher. For teachers the collaboration involved in clinical supervision means stripping the cloak of privacy from the decision-making rationale of teaching options.

The resultant nakedness of reasoning that previously has not been shared can produce some self-conscious awkwardness and accompanying discomfort.

It is reasonable to ask how many people in 'supervisory' positions in schools are genuinely prepared to give away the unilateral discretion of checking exactly how teaching should be altered? Is it possible that some supervisors see their job as telling teachers how to teach - and enjoying the credit for any resulting improvements? Could it be that some teachers are comfortable with the professional isolation they experience - and may resent exposing their thoughts and feelings about their teaching strategies and tactics? If such sentiments are plausible, then the suggestion that some educators may be unwilling participants in clinical supervision seems well-founded. Yet, willing participation is essential for the collaboration necessary for clinical supervision to occur. Such an observation underscores the need to prepare educators to participate in clinical supervision. More on that later.

Given a clear and compatible mission, given willing and prepared participation, clinical supervision may reach its potential - if adequate resources are committed to enable it. The primary resource, assuming prepared participants, is time, of course. Time is needed for preparation, for observation, for analysis of collected information, for conferences, and for assessing the clinical supervision program. Nor is the commitment of ample time sufficient - the time must be spent with an intensity and quality of interaction rich enough to justify its expenditure. Doing clinical supervision badly wastes valuable time and, as Cogan asserts, is worse than doing nothing at all.

While time is an important enabling resource for clinical supervision, coherent organisational communication patterns are no less crucial to successful clinical supervision. Schools very often send teachers mixed messages regarding their missions and their status. If, as one is trying to implement clinical supervision in a school, a curriculum planning committee is announcing a new and binding plan of study which few teachers helped design, and a teacher evaluator is defending the necessity for the old 'check-list' approach to assessing teacher performance, and staff development consists of three scattered days in which teachers attend a lecture on the topic of their choice, then any observer might conclude that either the mission for clinical supervision enjoyed less than enthusiastic support or that the school's approaches to improving teaching were co-ordinated by a committee of dubious sanity. Even when the leadership of a school has a sincere mission and secures willing participation, where time is provided, an infant clinical supervision program can be undermined by inconsistent messages - intended or not.

Preparation for Clinical Supervision

The first question is preparation for whom? Supervisors however they are determined within schools need skills and understandings to undertake clinical supervision adequately. Surprisingly, schools often seem to try a new clinical supervision program with supervisors who neither understand nor have the requisite skills. The results are not surprising. Very often, those who hold supervisory positions in schools have no preparation for observing teaching nor for conferring with teachers regarding classroom practice. Moreover, the emphasis in clinical supervision on disciplined inquiry with the accompanying commitment to reflective interaction requires abilities and dispositions not commonly associated with 'spot-check, see and tell' supervision. Therefore, supervisors need to be prepared for involvement in clinical supervision.

Nor should teachers be ignored in the preparation process. Experienced teachers who are accustomed to perfunctory visitation (if any at all) and proforma written summaries, may not be ready to plunge into a reflective assessment of their teaching practices - especially if they equate supervision with teacher evaluation wherein a supervisor passes judgement on the merit of their efforts. But what sort of preparation is needed?

Each school should have a clear expression of its purpose. Is its primary aim to increase student test scores? Is creativity among learners valued? Is preparing youth for active citizenship an important function? If so, how should teachers pursue this aim? It is interesting to speculate as to why these questions might be associated with preparing a school for clinical supervision.

Is it Practical?

Supervision requires reference points. Whether they are used by supervisors, teachers, learners, or others, reference points are needed to determine the value of existing practice or of a suggested alternative. There is no such entity as 'nonjudgmental' or 'value-free' supervision. A set of commonly understood 'planks' or position statements that clearly define desirable ends or means of school - a device that Sergiovanni and Starratt (1983) refer to as a school's espoused platform - can do much to provide these needed reference points.

As useful as it is, a school's espoused platform needs to be embellished with espoused platforms from individual teachers. The school platform expresses what the school stands for; the teacher's platform translates the more general school platform into a specific set of desired outcomes, preferred strategies and tactics, and views of learners and their roles in the teacher's classroom. It would be a mistake, however, to consider either platform as a set of enduring standards from which deviation is taboo. Reference points can, and should, change. When practices are encountered which seem incongruous with established platforms, reflective assessment may conclude that platforms need to be amended or revised, or that practices should change. By beginning preparation for clinical supervision with a deliberate attempt to formalise collective and individual platforms, the focus of supervisory attention is squarely fixed on learners.

Potential participants also need a clear understanding of the aims and procedures of clinical supervision itself. Other authors in this book, as well as Cogan (1973) and Goldhammer (1969; 1980), have described these eloquently. Disappointingly, the definitions of clinical supervision have become numerous - and varied. Some educators have come to define any practice which is based on descriptive information collected in a teacher's classroom as clinical supervision. Some, like Glatthorn (1984), suggest that clinical supervision is most appropriate for 'marginal' teachers. For some, clinical supervision is a check-list approach wherein supervisors inspect teachers' classrooms for frequency counts of 'effective' teaching practices and, based on these frequencies, recommend increasing or maintaining (I've never witnessed 'decreasing') the frequencies. Frankly, I find this practice appalling - at its worst it actually discourages reflection, substituting in its place a 'research says...' mentality that rejects contrary thinking - a dogmatic view the researchers themselves condemn.

However clinical supervision is defined, it should be clearly understood by all participants. If the original concept is accepted wherein good teachers are involved in collaborative and reflective assessment of teaching practices, then it is especially important that teachers and supervisors clearly reject from the outset that supervision is supposed to correct deficient teaching. Rather, all should grasp that clinical supervision is a way of intensely examining teaching practice, and its implications for learning. Moreover, the concept of clinical supervision is more likely to succeed with teachers who are competent.

What about the teacher who says: 'Fine. I understand what it is supposed to do, but what does it mean for my daily life?' Just as important as grasping the purpose for clinical supervision is developing clear expectations regarding its procedures. This may pose a more perplexing challenge for staff development people in schools, at least on the surface, because authors on clinical supervision typically offer differing versions of the components of a cycle. Does clinical supervision come in seven phases, five stages, or three steps? While different authors use differing labels and schemes, the functions of the cycle remain unaltered - the number of categories is simply a packaging decision.

To illustrate this point consider the five-part cycle illustrated in Table 7.1. The labels I use are deliberately chosen to differ from other authors' categories. The functions of each category differ little from the conception of clinical supervision offered by the original authors. Indeed, both Cogan (1973) and Goldhammer (1969) carefully explained that the mechanical sequence of events was less then sacred, and was to be varied when situational conditions warranted a differing approach. The point here is that participants in clinical supervision should understand the functions that comprise a cycle of supervision and the flexibility intended to tailor the cycle to fit individual circumstances.

TABLE 7.1
RELABELLED COMPONENTS OF A CLINICAL SUPERVISION CYCLE AND THEIR FUNCTIONS

Component	Functions
Readiness Conference	. to clarify intent of lesson to be observed . to clarify procedures for lesson to be observed . to clarify expected learner behaviour during lesson to be observed . to determine focus of observation and data collection strategies . to determine other relevant data sources . to determine schedule for remainder of cycle
Data Collection	. to record descriptive information in agreed upon fashion . to note in a descriptive manner any teacher or learner behaviour the supervisor considers especially noteworthy . to permit the supervisor to experience the lesson from the learner's perspective
Data Interpretation	. to enable both supervisor and teacher to examine collected information prior to the reflective conference . to identify recurring patterns or critical incidents among teacher or learner behaviours . to form tentative hypotheses relating teacher tactics to their consequences for learners

Reflective Conference	. to compare patterns and incidents identified by teacher and by supervisor during the preceding step . to compare perceptions of consequences of the observed lesson for learners . to link specific teaching tactics and moves to their hypothetical consequences for learners . to ponder aloud alternative tactics and moves and to consider their consequences for learners . to identify subsequent teaching strategies, tactics, and moves which seem likely to contribute to specific and desirable learner consequences . to consider data collection schemes appropriate for testing hypotheses formed as part of the preceding function
Cycle Evaluation	. to assess the consequences of the supervisory cycle for the teacher and, ultimately, for learners . to elicit the teacher's perceptions of helpful and not helpful supervisory strategies, tactics, and moves . to consider critically the teacher's responses to employed tactics and moves . for the supervisor to reflect upon the present professional relationship with the teacher as it was manifested during the cycle . for the supervisor to consider the possible effects of alternative strategies, tactics, and moves

- to plan modifications for subsequent cycles
- for the supervisor to form plans to test attractive hypotheses generated during the preceding function

---

Simply examining a cross-section of a single cycle is helpful, but not sufficient to convey the procedures of clinical supervision. Prospective participants need to consider the rationale for repetitive cycles of observation and conferral, and how the ongoing sequence of cycles interacts functionally with the individual cycles. When a teacher participates in a sporadic and infrequent program of classroom visitation and conferral, there is a sense of finality that is a delusion. Not so in clinical supervision. Because observations and conferences in early cycles will lead to subsequent activity, they need not attempt to resolve all issues or attain closure. For the same reason that expectations for reading a chapter of a larger book differ greatly from reading a short story, anticipated events for a round of supervision differ when that round is part of an ongoing effort, than when it stands alone. Not only does the cyclic approach to clinical supervision permit the development of 'experienced-eye' observations and of colleagial, familiar interpersonal communication, it also allows for the development and testing of hypotheses regarding the differing consequences of alternative teaching tactics.

Prospective participants must also understand that clinical supervision is not another 'quick-fix' approach to improving teaching - more the antithesis. While the illusion of 'quick-fix' is appealing to outside reformers, history clearly shows the appeal to be a mirage. Participants in clinical supervision must anticipate one cycle will be unlike another. Where one may generate a hypothesis regarding the effects of exposing learners to small group discussions, the next may trial that hypothesis, and another may test the same hypothesis with a different structure to the group. After prospective participants have some appreciation and understanding of the aims and procedures of clinical supervision, there is a need for some skills necessary to do the job. To be able to carry out the functions outlined in

Table 7.1, supervisors need to be able to draw pertinent information from teachers; to design and carry out meaningful data collection strategies; to recognise patterns and incidents in teaching and learning actions which pertain to learning; to assist teachers to compare intended consequences of a lesson with both school and individual platforms; to assist teachers to predict and reflect upon consequences of teaching for particular learners; and, to help teachers identify and test alternative teaching tactics which seem likely to enhance student learning in some predictable fashion. Clearly, this is a demanding list of 'minimal' needs. To develop skills consistent with these needs requires more than a two-hour workshop. More specifically, supervisors need skills in interpersonal communication, collecting information through observation, and hypothesis formation and testing to go with their knowledge of effective teaching, of the norms and expectations of the community, and of the school's and the teacher's espoused platforms. One approach for developing this knowledge and skill is discussed later. Suffice to say here that clinical supervision requires as Garman (1982) has pointed out, skilled service. When one attempts clinical supervision with an unskilled supervisor, the results are much the same as when one attempts to perform surgery with an unskilled physician. (One might argue that there should be no unskilled physicians - an interesting parallel.)

Although a lack of preparation for supervisors is often a problem in initiating a clinical supervision program, the lack of preparation of teachers is even more prevalent. If clinical supervision is to be collaborative in deed as well as in rhetoric, then some preparation for the collaborating teachers seems crucial. The need for specific information regarding purpose, procedures, and expectations has already been examined. But, does a teacher who participates in clinical supervision require any special skills? To phrase the question another way, if collaboration is truly desired, and if collaboration is indeed rare in schools, and if collaboration is a form of human interaction requiring some skills, isn't it reasonable to prepare teachers to employ these skills?

Introducing a Clinical Supervision Program

Given all of this reasoning it is an interesting question as to how one begins a clinical supervision program? In a word, slowly! Without wanting to be in any way prescriptive experience has taught me that there are a few guiding principles. Naturally, they do not apply in all situations and the reader is free to adopt or vary them in whatever way is necessary.

(a) Start on a Small Scale

There is truth in the old adage: to attempt too much is to do nothing well? The most common flaw when schools move to clinical supervision is to try too much too soon. Instead of trying to work with fifteen or more different teachers at once, there is merit in beginning with two or three. It also makes sense to start with two or three of the best teachers so that the message that supervision is not just for poor teachers is quickly communicated and so that the neophyte clinical supervisor has access to valuable feedback. After all, it's much easier to develop collaborative efforts with capable teachers. Once the new clinical supervisor has the experience of collaborative problem-solving with resourceful teachers, knowledge and confidence are gained which can facilitate dealing with other teachers. Starting as it were, in a 'greenhouse,' on a small scale with the best of conditions and resources increases the probability of early success. Not only does initial success contribute to the supervisor's confidence, it also increases the likelihood that teachers will consider their own participation in the process more positively.

(b) Provide a Thorough Orientation to All Participants

Time invested in getting all participants to express and clarify platforms, to understand the purposes and procedures of clinical supervision, and to develop communication and collective problem-solving skills pays dividends. It is when all participants participate in platform development and refinement, that a 'common cause' cements collective effort.

It is also true that when all participants clearly understand the aims and means of clinical supervision, each is better able to assess pilot efforts and pinpoint successes and failures in the process. While supervisors may not be accustomed to having knowledgeable teachers analyse and constructively criticise supervisory practices, when it occurs it models an openness to collaborate on refining practice which clinical supervision expects of teachers, while promoting a reciprocity of service that is likely to facilitate mutual respect and a productive working relationship.

Finally, the development of communication and problem setting and problem solving skills, facilitates understanding and overcomes barriers to collective efforts such as defensiveness and problem avoidance. Preparation for this does not prevent communication breakdowns but it does give participants a greater ability to recognise and deal with these obstacles as they occur.

(c) Publicise the Reason for and Nature of the Pilot Program to all Teachers

The impression that some teachers in the school are receiving special treatment may create unnecessary problems and tensions among non-participants. The time and effort of ensuring that all teachers understand what the pilot is and why only a few people are participating, alleviates many of the anxieties and misunderstandings. Above all, it avoids the problem of non-participants inventing their own distorted understanding of what is really happening.

(d) Work to Understand Teaching from the Teacher's Perspective

This doesn't mean abandoning or concealing personal views about teaching; only that they should not be imposed on teachers. It should go without saying that any time any educator sees professionally negligent behaviour, she/he is obliged to correct it. But truly negligent behaviour is rare in schools. More often educators are likely to disagree on teaching strategies or tactics. In these cases, especially in the early stages of a clinical supervision program, the appropriate focus is on the goal itself. Is it being achieved or not? Could it be achieved better? If so, how would we know? What indicators of success are we willing to accept? Questions such as these focus attention on the learners - rather than on our pet tactics or opinions per se.

Is it Practical?

The initial question to be pursued is how the supervisor can help the teacher attain his or her goals. Assuming the teacher has some worthy goals, clarifying those goals and their relationship to the school's mission (through the platform development discussed earlier) and focussing on concerns of the teacher in early cycles seems prudent. Even if those concerns seem trivial to the supervisor, they are worth heeding in the interests of collaboration. Very often teachers suggest initial attention be focussed on students' actions during classroom observation. As long as teachers accept that their job is to influence what students do, this is a perfectly acceptable, even advantageous, early focus. Whether or not students are behaving in a desirable fashion, descriptive information about them provides a rich base for reflection.

(e) Analysing Positive Teaching Patterns and Moves

If every time the supervisor asks a question about an aspect of teaching, it turns out to be because she/he thinks it inappropriate, the teacher soon learns that when something is targeted for a question, the supervisor is really saying, 'You could have done that better, now, couldn't you? Such patterns can make for highly defensive and non-productive conferences. By focussing a series of questions squarely on the prominent strength perceived in their teaching, teachers' assessments of their own efficacy can be elicited. If the intent is to promote teacher self-assessment, teachers should be encouraged to focus on the consequences of their teaching - especially when those consequences are all they were supposed to be. In this way teachers can get practice relating learner effects to teaching strategies and tactics - and get a feeling of deserved accomplishment. In a job where such 'glows' are seldom shared with colleagues, this may be a major benefit of clinical supervision for teachers. At a time when good teachers are more likely to leave teaching than their less effective counterparts, the payoff to a school may be quite tangible.

(f) Monitor your Clinical Supervision Program

The importance of collecting evidence on the strengths and shortcomings of clinical supervision and of supervisors' practices, especially during a pilot can hardly be overstated. The reason for this is simply integrity. Clinical supervision calls upon teachers to expose their own performance to collective examination and to reflective assessment.

How does one evaluate a clinical supervision program? There are several worthy sources of information, such as : records of time spent in observations and conferences; teachers' opinions regarding the helpfulness of the supervision; supervisors' success stories; perhaps even measures of student performance. One rather easy piece of information to collect is the teachers' compilation of what they do differently now that can be at least partly attributed to their participation in a clinical supervision program. When this result is combined with their appraisal as to how these changes have affected their students, one has a crude, but I think valid, indication of clinical supervision's contribution.

Another indicator of the success of a clinical supervision pilot is the extent to which teachers involved in the pilot advocate participation to others. If these teachers voluntarily espouse the virtues of participating in clinical supervision with all its time demands, then the pilot has succeeded. If not, then the supervisor should carefully examine her/his strategies and tactics, form alternatives which offer the hope of better results, and test the most attractive of these with a second pilot.

The Last Part

The intent of this chapter has been to examine the practicality of clinical supervision. The approach has been through the question - practical for what? It was shown that a local mission for supervising teachers needed to be matched to the aims for clinical supervision. If the missions were not compatible, then clinical supervision was suggested as not being practicable for that site at that time. There was seen to be a need to examine the likelihood for willing participation after ample preparation. If local supervisors or teachers are not going to begin cycles willingly, then clinical supervision is not practical. Ample resources need to exist to provide supervisors and teachers with time to participate in clinical supervision and in preparation for it - and to design and deliver adequate preparation for and reasonable implementation of clinical supervision. If not, then to proceed is folly. If all these conditions are positive, then clinical supervision is likely to be practical <u>if approached wisely</u>.

A wise approach includes preparation, including practice, for both supervisors and teachers; clarification of both school and individual platforms; a 'greenhouse' introduction involving only a few able and voluntary participants; a willingness to adapt plans and procedures to fit the needs of the setting and of the participants; and a commitment to collect evaluative information about the clinical supervision program. Given all these qualifications, clinical supervision is clearly practical.

However, this last part includes more than a summary. It includes the only mention of the single ingredient most important to the practicality of clinical supervision in any site. An indispensable prerequisite to introducing clinical supervision as a practical and valuable service is an on-site leader who believes in it. The belief alone is sufficient to get clinical supervision started - but leadership is needed to get it started right. Without such a person, an advocate with the ability to lead, clinical supervision is not practical.

REFERENCES

Cogan, M., <u>Clinical Supervision</u>, Boston: Houghton Miffin, 1973

Garman, N., The clinical approach to supervision, In T. Sergiovanni (ed), <u>Supervision of Teaching</u>, Alexandria, Va: Yearbook of the Association of Supervision & Curriculum Development, 1982

Glatthorn, A., <u>Differentiated Supervision</u>, Alexandria, Va: Association for Supervision & Curriculum Development, 1984

Goldhammer, R., <u>Clinical Supervision : Special Methods for the Supervision of Teachers</u>, New York: Holt, Rinehart & Winston, 1969

Goldhammer, R., Anderson, R., & Krajewski, R., <u>Clinical Supervision: Special Methods for the Supervision of Teachers</u>, 2nd ed., New York: Holt, Rinehart & Winston, 1980

Sergiovanni, T., & Starratt, R., <u>Supervision: Human Perspectives</u>, (3rd ed), New York: McGraw Hill, 1983

AUTHOR INDEX

SUBJECT INDEX

NOTTINGHAM
UNIVERSITY LIBRARY